Black Irish
White Jamaican

Black Irish
White Jamaican

my family's journey

NIAMH O'BRIEN

author HOUSE®

AuthorHouse™ LLC
1663 Liberty Drive
Bloomington, IN 47403
www.authorhouse.com
Phone: 1-800-839-8640

Published by AuthorHouse   07/26/2013

ISBN: 978-1-4817-7077-4 (sc)
ISBN: 978-1-4817-6801-6 (hc)
ISBN: 978-1-4817-7076-7 (e)

Library of Congress Control Number: 2013911576

CONTENTS

DISCLAIMER

I have written a story that is, to the best of my recollection, honest and true. I have not changed any names or facts, so I apologize to anyone who finds inaccuracies in dates, names or events. I also apologize to anyone who disagrees with my critical comments and political conclusions, I respect our differences. If I have offended anyone for any reason, I apologize. I just wanted to tell my family's story.

THE AUTHOR

"Happy Family"—1957

DEDICATION

For my Mom. Thank you for your sacrifices, your endurance and your loving heart. You will always be my inspiration and your spirit will be with me forever.

Maeve O'Brien—1950

CHAPTER 1

We're not in Ireland anymore

Tom And Maeve O'Brien before leaving Ireland—1950

If my grandfather had had his way on that cold January day in 1951, my mother would have never set foot on that ship for a seasick-prone journey that would ferry her far away from her native Ireland. Fortunately, or perhaps unfortunately, he had no say in the matter. Mom, twenty-one and already married with a two-year-old son, was six-months pregnant with me and making the long journey across the Atlantic to join my father in that "godforsaken place" (my grandfather's words). As she found herself on the docks of Dublin, about to leave her safe, sheltered life, she had no clue that she was about to embark on a roller-coaster adventure that would last over thirty years.

That "godforsaken place" was actually the hot, sizzling, tropical island of Jamaica.

My grandfather, Peter Daly, had already lost his son Paddy to Australia a few years earlier, and as it turned out, he was never to see Paddy again, nor meet any of his six Australian grandchildren. He felt an ache in the pit of his stomach as he watched his beloved daughter Maeve also prepare to sail out of his life. He could detect the mixture of both fear and wonder in her eyes, but knew he was helpless to stop what was about to happen. He was painfully aware that his influence in her life was almost over.

"I am so sorry that I can only go with you as far as Southampton" he told her in his thick Irish brogue. "You'll be on your own for the crossing of the Atlantic. Do you think you'll be able to manage?" He was truly worried about her.

"I think I can, Daddy, but I would feel so much better if you were coming with me the whole way."

Even if she didn't want to go, my mother actually had no say in this life-altering journey, as my father had already accepted a position managing a large canning factory in Kingston, Jamaica's capital. He had traveled ahead (in comfort by plane) to arrange accommodations for his young family, leaving his wife to make the long, exhausting journey alone. I want to believe this was not a deliberately thoughtless act on his part, just poor planning.

In spite of a deeply rooted Irish heritage, for my father, the opportunity to start afresh in a new country was an exciting adventure of mammoth proportions. It was the chance to escape the repressed, post–World War II Ireland and build a better life for himself and his family on a warm, exotic Caribbean island. My mother didn't see her future in quite the same light. She had barely travelled outside of Dublin, much less Ireland, and was naïve as to the ways of the world. But her destiny had been sealed. Besides, she would have followed my father anywhere then.

As Mom and my young brother Peter boarded that ship in Southampton, she looked back at her heartbroken father waving good-bye from the dock, apprehension building inside her. She was leaving behind everything that was familiar to her: her friends, her family, and her Irish way of life. She had no way of knowing what lay ahead, which was probably a good thing, because if she had, she might never have stepped on board that ship. All she knew was that her journey had begun. Was it bravery or ignorance? Surely it had to be a little of both. She was taking a huge leap of faith as she headed toward the strange, foreign country she would soon call home.

My mother, Maeve Daly, was a stunning Irish beauty with long auburn hair and beautiful blue eyes. She was petite, gentle, and soft-spoken, often referred to by her siblings as "the delicate beauty." Although her life had been somewhat sheltered, she was outgoing and popular among her peers. She had a large following of loyal friends who loved life and, like most Irish people I know, always seemed to know how to have a good time.

Both of her parents came from West Cork, a majestic area on the southwest coast of Ireland. My grandfather, Peter Daly, was my grandmother's second husband. He came from a large farming family, and my grandmother, Bridget Keane, came from a family of mostly professionals—teachers, doctors, and lawyers. An unlikely combination, those two, but they seemed to have a lot of friends in common, and more importantly, they shared the same political ideology and both were Catholic. When they met, which was around 1924, the country was still recovering from the 1916 uprising against England and the

Irish War of Independence that followed. The Irish Republican Army (IRA) was formed at this time to spearhead the revolution. Both my grandparents supported the IRA then. The war was brutal and bloody, but in the end, two-thirds of Ireland won independence from the British, who had governed and controlled the country for over seven hundred years. Unfortunately, the war did not end there. In 1922, when England decided it wanted to keep six counties in the north of Ireland for themselves, a civil war broke out in Ireland. Half the population was willing to compromise and allow Northern Ireland to remain under British rule, but the other half wanted total independence from Britain.

Back then in Ireland, and even today, sharing the same political ideology about the fate of Northern Ireland was crucial to maintaining any kind of loyal friendship. You either supported the British rule of Northern Ireland or you were vehemently against it. No Irish family survived that war without developing passionate feelings for one side or the other. Today, my observation is that only the Protestant population of Northern Ireland is totally comfortable with British rule, while the Catholic population in the North and the South are still angry and resentful about it. Things have quieted down a lot since the turn of the twenty-first century, but sadly, this has happened only after suffering through many decades of bitter fighting between the two sides.

In 1922, toward the end of the civil war, a shocking tragedy occurred. My grandmother's husband, John Cotter, was ambushed and murdered by the IRA as he was walking home from work. The men who shot him later admitted it was a case of mistaken identity, and they wrote a deeply apologetic letter to my grandmother, but that did not take away the pain or huge void this horrific event left in her life. What was even worse, her two sons, Billy and Noel, who were very young at the time, witnessed the murder, and although people around the scene tried to shield them, both sons saw their father's bullet-ridden body lying in a pool of blood in the middle of the street. This was a traumatizing experience for everyone in the family but especially for my poor grandmother who was left as a young widow with three small children to raise on her own: Billy, Noel, and a three-year-old daughter, Maureen.

It is amazing to me how, under the guise of war, unforgivable heartbreaking events can occur, and somehow all sense of accountability is ignored. In peace time, these men would have been tried for murder, but sadly, because there was a civil war going on, there were no consequences, just a terrible loss. It is unbelievable to me how war can warp a man's conscience into excusing and forgiving inhumane behavior—just a sad observation on my part.

Meanwhile, all during the war Peter Daly had been a staunch supporter of the revolution against England and a good friend of Michael Collins, one of the heroes and leaders of the uprising. They were both from West Cork. Unfortunately, Michael Collins was also ambushed and murdered by his fellow Irishmen during the civil war. I believe that if Michael Collins had not been assassinated, he would probably have been independent Ireland's first leader. This was another reminder of how horrific events during war time can change lives forever. Even after Michael's untimely death, Peter Daly always remained friends with the Collins family.

As fate would have it, my grandmother Bridget Keane Cotter, was a school teacher and worked with the sister of Michael Collins, Margaret Collins O'Driscoll. They became especially close after they both had loved ones killed in the "troubles"—as the war was called—my grandmother losing her husband, and Margaret losing her brother. After the war was over, and things had gone back to some kind of normalcy, Margaret Collins O'Driscoll loved to have friends and family over on Sunday afternoons. I am told it was at one of those Sunday afternoon gatherings that my grandparents, Bridget Keane Cotter and Peter Daly, met. I would like to add "and fell in love," but I hesitate because according to my aunt Maureen, they never truly fell in love. She always suspected it was just a marriage of convenience. But whatever the reason, they did get married. I am sure my grandmother was only too happy to find a bachelor brave enough to take on her three young children. Together they had two more children, my mother Maeve, whom my grandfather absolutely adored, and Paddy, who, unfortunately, always had a bit of a tumultuous relationship with his father. (Maybe that was why Paddy headed off to Australia at the tender age of nineteen.)

My grandfather also loved his three stepchildren, Billy, Noel, and Maureen, and although Noel was always a bit unstable and often tested his stepfather's patience, Peter Daly was good to all his children. I think Noel never really recovered from witnessing the murder of his father. He grew up physically, but emotionally he was stuck somewhere in his childhood, which, I am told, can happen if you have been traumatized at a young age. Consequently, his behavior was often totally outrageous and immature, resulting in frequent headaches and heartaches for his parents. I could write another book about Noel's antics, but for now, I can give you a tiny taste of how unstable he was. During World War II, he joined every possible army that would take him, and he was thrown out of every possible army that took him, including the US Army. You know he must have been pretty bad, because during World War II they were holding on to every enlistee they could get. In spite of the challenges Noel put him through, Peter Daly remained faithful to my grandmother his entire life, so they must have had something good to hang on to.

Castle Salem, Rosscarbery, West Cork, Ireland.

The Family Farm and Castle

My grandfather, Peter, was born in a farmhouse in Rosscarbery, West Cork that has quite an interesting background. He was the eleventh of fourteen children born into the Daly family and was subjected to the traditions of rural Ireland where the eldest son inherits the farm and everyone born after him gets diddlysquat. So my grandfather, having many brothers born before him, got diddlysquat. Thankfully, he was a very smart man and studied hard, going on to have a successful career with the Ministry of Agriculture in Dublin and proving to be a very good provider for his new family. Maybe my grandmother knew what she was doing after all when she agreed to marry him.

Even though the eldest granduncle's branch of the family inherited the Daly farm and all the land, I have had the opportunity to visit this wonderful old property many times. Today, my second cousin, Peter Daly, who is named after my grandfather, still makes a good living from the land. The actual farmhouse is over 350 years old and shares a common wall with Castle Salem, an old castle that dates back to the 1040s. You can open a door in the cozy carpeted farmhouse, step through, and find yourself in middle of the ruins of this eleventh-century building. It feels as if you are traveling through a time machine. Except for the roof, the castle, for the most part, is still intact. You can see where the sink in the kitchen was and identify a hole where leftovers were thrown down a shoot, landing in a trough outside for the pigs to feast on. You can also see where the toilets were on each floor of the old castle. They were built of stone in the shape of a square seat with a hole in the middle and emptied directly to the ground far below. On each level, the toilet was two feet away from the one above it, so the waste would not fall onto the floor below but travel straight through to the ground. Apparently, they used moss for toilet paper. I find it quite amazing that the castle had not only an eleventh-century version of a garbage disposal in the kitchen but also indoor plumbing. Very civilized for the time, especially remembering my young experiences in Ireland in the 1950s of being sent to an outhouse in the middle of the backyard to use the toilet.

Another interesting thing about the family farmhouse was that it was built in the only Quaker community in all of Ireland, and apparently

William Penn, the founder of Pennsylvania, was a Quaker, and he would stay there when he went back to Ireland on visits. I am told I actually slept in the same bedroom as Penn. Although the floor now slants about five degrees, it is a solid old house and a unique place to visit. My granduncle's branch of the family always welcomes my family to the farm with open arms. I love going there and visit as often as I can. Knowing that my grandfather, my great-grandfather, and my great-great-grandfather were all born in that very house, I often hope to connect with them in some way. I have never actually gotten in touch with any of the spirits of these ancestors, but the experiences on the family farm have given me great insight into my mother's strong Irish heritage.

My father, Tom O'Brien, was a strikingly good-looking Irishman. He had a thick head of wavy black hair and deep blue eyes. He played every possible sport, so his body was one of an athlete, firm and muscular. Tom was born into a large middle-class family that originated in the city of Belfast, Northern Ireland. The O'Briens were hard-working people who lived in the middle of the Catholic neighborhood in this Protestant-governed city. Dad's father, William, was a serious man who fought hard in the war of independence against England and was an active member of the IRA during the uprising in 1916. He was captured and tortured by the British during the war. A gruesome experience I am sure. All Irish people have heard the many horrific stories of torture and heroism that came out of that war, mostly told through haunting Irish ballads that are indelibly embedded into the memory of every patriot and sung in pubs all over Ireland, even today. Somehow, and very thankfully, my grandfather William O'Brien, managed to escape from the British, and when he did, the family quickly found themselves moving to Dublin. He died in his forties, so I never knew him. Neither my grandmother nor any of her children ever spoke about what happened during those years— sometimes war is too painful to talk about.

After the war was over and the South finally won its freedom from England, life settled down for the O'Briens. My grandfather worked in a fish market and earned just enough money to get by, but at least the family always had a steady diet of fresh fish. When he died, the IRA had a full military funeral for him. This was quite a shock to his wife and family, who had no idea why he deserved such honor. I think it was best that they did not know the details of their father's duties as an IRA soldier during the war. For all we know, he might have been part of the plot to assassinate my step-grandfather, John Cotter—a terrible thought that would not surprise me in the slightest. My grandmother always said she would have much preferred to be compensated with some kind of widow's pension from the IRA instead of an expensive funeral. My grandfather O'Brien had left his family penniless, so all the children who were of age had to go out and earn an income to keep the family going. This included my father, who at age fifteen was helping support his mother and four younger brothers. The family was strong though, and they made it through just fine. My grandmother, Jane O'Brien, although widowed at a young age, continued to live a simple but comfortable life, remaining in Dublin until she died at the age of ninety-five.

Dad seemed totally unaffected by his father's militant past and stern outlook on life. Instead, he was always full of fun and adventure, a man with boundless energy and humorous high spirits. He was gentle, kind, and hugely generous, but at the same time, he could be wild, reckless, and totally irresponsible. When he met my mother, he was only twenty-one, but he fell madly in love with her, and according to my aunt Maureen, my mother felt the same passionate love for him. Maybe they were a bit too passionate, as Mom found herself pregnant at the tender age of eighteen. This was quite a dilemma in the conservative Ireland of the 1940s, so a quick marriage was arranged. I am guessing they would have married regardless, as they did truly seem to love one another. And so there they were—two young people about to break away from their deeply rooted Irish families and pioneer an adventure of their own, miles away from home in the warm Caribbean.

The voyage across the Atlantic was grueling for my mother. She became so nauseous that she could not leave her cabin for ten days. The ship was comfortable but did not have many passengers on board, so after a few days all knew of Maeve O'Brien's plight and were getting worried about her. The staff was doing a good job of keeping my brother occupied during the day, but concerns grew with every passing hour that my mother could not eat nor hold liquids down. Finally, Mrs. Hearne, an English doctor's wife who was also making the journey to Jamaica to join her husband, went to my mother's cabin and took matters into her own hands.

"Now my dear," she told my mother in her cultured British accent, "I am getting you dressed, and we are going up to the deck to get some fresh air." Refusing to take no for an answer, she reminded my mother, "You're going to lose that baby if you don't eat."

Mrs. Hearne got my mother up out of bed, dressed her, and put her in a chair on deck. She did not leave her side until my mother slowly started recovering. No one knew at the time, but her pregnancy had triggered the onset of a lifelong illness that would not be properly diagnosed until four years later. Mrs. Hearne probably saved my mother's life on that voyage.

Maeve, Peter and Mrs. Hearne on the deck of BAYANO

Maeve somehow survived the long Atlantic crossing but arrived on the sweltering docks of Jamaica dazed and weak. Unprepared for what awaited her, my mother stepped out of the peaceful surroundings of the passenger ship into overwhelming culture shock on the docks of Kingston. She was immediately hit by a wall of heat so oppressive she often described it as walking into an oven. Every breath was an effort. Her body broke out into a continuous flow of sweat that couldn't be squelched. Then the noise and pandemonium hit. It seemed that hundreds of young black men were swarming around to carry the many trunks, suitcases, boxes, and various other pieces of luggage that were hauled across the Atlantic by the ships' passengers—most of whom were white. Up to this point in her life, the only black people Mom had ever seen were the royal princes who were sent from Africa to finish their education at prestigious Trinity College in Dublin. Those black students were very wealthy and were always regally dressed in traditional African garb. When spotted walking around Dublin, they had a mystique about them that caused much curiosity from the all-white population of Dublin. The chaos at the port of Kingston was a different scene entirely. The crowds of men were shabbily dressed, some even without shoes, and all were shouting at the same time in an incomprehensible accent, hoping to get a few pence for carrying luggage to the waiting vehicles. Looking around, all she could see was a sea of black faces. Even after years of living in Jamaica, whenever she returned from a visit to Ireland, it still took an adjustment period to get used to the stark contrast in her surroundings. This first experience of arriving in Jamaica, however, was the most overwhelming, and much to her relief, she finally spotted my father waiting on the dock to take her out of the melee.

"Maeve, Maeve. Over here!" Dad yelled exuberantly over the crowd. He could not contain his excitement as he welcomed my mother to her new home.

"What do you think, isn't this place wonderful?" he asked her. "Did you see all the palm trees and beaches, and isn't the sunshine just brilliant?" (Everything always seemed "brilliant" to my father). It was pretty obvious that in just a few short weeks he had already fallen madly in love with this exotic island.

His wife, however, did not have the energy to share his enthusiasm. Collapsing into his arms, she told him, "I have never been more relieved to see you." Mom was too exhausted to notice the palm trees or the beaches or to appreciate the brilliant sunshine. Her clothes were soaked in perspiration, and the beads of sweat rolling down her face were relentless.

"Does my bed have a fan over it?" was the only thing she wanted to know. All she could think about was collapsing into bed, curling up with a soft pillow, and somehow cooling off her body.

The ride through the streets of Kingston was harrowing. The roads were narrow, filthy, and full of potholes. Animals and people alike seemed to meander out into the streets whenever they pleased. Goats, cows, donkeys, chickens, cyclists, and children were all obstacles that took great skill to avoid. As the car made its way through the winding roads toward their small rental apartment, I am sure my mother was wondering what she had gotten herself into.

Mom never spoke much about those first few months in Jamaica, maybe because she had been in a permanent daze and did not recall most of it. The only story I do remember her telling me was her first encounter with a Jamaican flying cockroach. Apparently this happened on her very first night in Jamaica and ended with my father running around the bedroom, a shoe in one hand, trying desperately to swat the unwelcome visitor as my mother, in a state of panic, huddled under the bedcovers. She was so traumatized by the experience that it left an indelible mark in her memory. Even though she would encounter many nasty insects over the years, she never ever got used to the cockroaches. I remember seeing them fly through the house frequently while growing up. If one came anywhere near my mother's head she would start screaming and batting her hands wildly in the air in a frenzy.

Even though I know no other details of the very early days in Jamaica, it became obvious to me that my mother must have panicked a lot, sweated a lot, wept a lot, slept a lot, and probably pondered a lot about the validity of my father's decision to move his family halfway across the world to this sweltering tropical island.

As she awaited my birth, Maeve Daly O'Brien developed levels of tolerance and patience that would last her a lifetime. I believe that, unfortunately, this is when she started to settle for a life of low expectations, something she gave into too easily in my opinion. Having complete faith in my father, and being passionately in love with him, she simply and quickly relinquished control of her life. I suppose this was only natural at the time, as most women of Mom's generation relied on their husbands for everything. Her generation was wedged between the traditional past and the independent future. At the beginning of her marriage, she definitely leaned toward the traditional past. It was assumed that husbands would live up to their financial responsibilities to support their wives and families and would certainly always remain faithful in the marriage. Unrealistic expectations for today's society maybe, but in Ireland, in the 1940s, it was generally a safe bet.

The only exception might have been if "the drink" was involved, although even then, it would never have led to separation in a marriage. Come to think of it, "the drink" was often symptomatic of an unhappy marriage and it was the only outlet the Irish had for escaping their misery. After all, there was no such thing as divorce in Ireland at the time. Divorce did not become legal until the 1990s. If you were unhappy in your marriage, you went to the pub to drown your misery. No one would ever consider divorce.

My mother, even though coming from a family of strong professional women—doctors lawyers, and university professors who all earned substantial incomes and were advanced for their time—never followed in their footsteps. Instead, she opted for the role of subservient wife. I guess I have always been puzzled by this, especially with such strong female role models to emulate. Why, in her marriage, did she relinquish control to my father so readily? If she could have foreseen the future, I am sure she'd never have let the balance of power get so one-sided and out of whack.

My birth in Jamaica, in 1951, automatically made me a citizen of this small Caribbean island. In later years, this caused me quite an identity crisis as I was often called both a black Irish (my Celtic coloring of black hair and blue eyes and fair skin) and a white Jamaican (for obvious reasons). My mother, father, and older brother, on the other hand, were always foreigners, and although my father embraced Jamaica as his home, he still ended up under the unwelcomed title of *expat* during the entire time he lived there.

I am not sure if my parents made the right choice by immigrating to Jamaica, but I know my father thought so. Expat notwithstanding, to his delight he came to discover when living in a third-world country, as Jamaica was, and being white, educated, and charming, as my father was, you were inevitably thrown into a life of privilege and status that you would never have found back home. In Ireland, he was a small fish in a big pond (maybe a minnow). White, good-looking, educated men were a dime a dozen there, but in Jamaica, where white, good-looking, educated men were scarce, he became a big fish (yes, I would say an orca whale) in a small pond, and he loved every minute of it. In fact, on many an occasion, this phenomenon caused him to have bouts of temporary amnesia, where he forgot he even had a wife, much less a family, resulting in much anguish and pain for my mother.

To outsiders, our lives looked glamorous and enviable, especially to our relatives back in Ireland. We lived in a warm, tropical country and had many servants and great opportunities. But as exciting and interesting as life seemed in Jamaica, living there was scary and presented many crazy challenges. Third-world countries are prone to violent crime and political unrest, all of which were dangers we experienced. Would my mother have preferred to live a secure but routine life in Ireland? Did she regret the thirty unsettling years she stuck it out with my father in Jamaica? I will never know. Maeve O'Brien came from the generation of high tolerance and tight lips, and she never shared unhappy feelings with her children.

What I do know is that she had one of the most interesting and challenging lives of anyone I know. If Mom had not stayed in Jamaica, I would not be able to share some of my most intriguing stories with you, many of which I experienced with her. It was a life full of contradictions. There were fun-loving adventures mixed with terrifying encounters, strong friendships mixed with painful betrayal, and an overactive social life, met with, at times, deep loneliness. The extreme high and lows were unsettling but never dull. We actually had breakfast with Queen Elizabeth's relative Princess Alice one morning and later shared a patty (meat pie) with a woman who was so poor she did not own a pair of shoes—both in the same day. Such was life in the Caribbean.

Scenic Newcastle, above Irish Town
Photo©Cookie Kinkead

CHAPTER 2

Never underestimate the power of a hurricane

After the initial culture shock of moving to this strange, overheated island, my mother tried hard to adjust. She did get her wish of a whirring fan over her bed. Other than that, in the '50s in Jamaica, the veranda was the only other place you might find a slight breeze to help you cool down. The cooling system Mom resorted to the most was a simple handheld fan that almost never left her hand. I have vivid memories, even into my teens, of my mother tirelessly fanning her face and neck with a colorful fan, which she seemed to have an endless supply of. This cooling method was not her first choice, of course, but it was her only choice at the time, as these days were long before the arrival of air conditioning in Jamaica.

To help tolerate the oppressive heat, my father decided to move us to a little village high in the mountains called Irish Town. Maybe he thought my mother would feel a little bit more at home there, although the only thing Irish about Irish Town was the name. However, it was then, and still is today, one of the most idyllic places in all of Jamaica.

The village was nestled in the magnificent Blue Mountains, surrounded by panoramic views of the capitol city of Kingston below and the Caribbean Sea in the distance. The Blue Mountains are famous to non-Jamaicans for some of the best coffee beans in the world. But to Jamaicans, the Blue Mountains are also known for their rainforest-like landscape that is, without a doubt, breathtakingly beautiful. The perfect climate and fertile soil produce expansive canopies of tall, deep-green trees and lush vegetation of all types, including the well-known *ganja* (marijuana). Many small streams pop out from the side of the mountain, growing quickly into fast-moving rivers that become spectacular waterfalls as they seek the quickest path to the sea far below. Added to the scenic majesty of the greenery and the rivers are some of the most vibrant tropical flowers that nature could possibly produce—flowers of all shapes and colors. Every view from Amberly, our new rented house, encompassed bright-orange Poinciana trees, vibrant red and pink bougainvillea, yellow frangipani, hibiscus of all colors, and many other exotic flowers whose names I still do not know.

Needless to say, the area was a mystical place of spectacular beauty. I have a sad feeling, however, that my mother was too overwhelmed to appreciate any of Irish Town's unique splendors. I know for a fact though that she did appreciate the much cooler climate that the Blue Mountains offered. In addition to the improved weather, the greatest thing about Amberly was that the most wonderful, caring woman in the world lived there—my nanny, Ella. Ella fell on her knees and praised God several times when she saw the arrival of a tiny baby at the house. Sweeping me up in her arms, she carried me away, and I don't think my mother saw much of her daughter after that. Ella thought unequivocally that I was a gift from God bestowed directly to her.

"Tank yu, lawd Jesus, mi priors dem have been hanswered," she repeated, over and over in her native *patois*. Apparently, she had been praying for years for a baby to care for, and I was the answer to those prayers. Ella was a gift to me also, as Mom's health started to deteriorate rapidly after giving birth. She got very weak, lost a lot of weight, and spent many days in and out of the hospital. The puzzling illness was again rearing its ugly head, but the doctors could not give her any insight as to what was causing it. During this time, I was blessed to have Ella's nurturing arms to care for me.

Ella and Niamh 1952

It was Ella who was to get us through one of the worst hurricanes to hit Jamaica in fifty years. It was August, and we had been in Jamaica for seven months. Except for the constant feeling of weakness, shortages of food, regular power outages, water shortages, nerve-racking transportation challenges, a bout of whooping cough, and mosquitoes, cockroaches, and various other bugs, my mother was settling in quite well. Then, on one bright sunny August day, word reached Irish Town that a hurricane was approaching Jamaica. People only had twenty-four hours warning in those days, and warnings were communicated by telegraph sent from post office to post office. After receiving the news, each post office would fly a hurricane flag from its roof top, letting the villagers know a storm was eminent.

My mother did not really know what a hurricane was, but having lived in Ireland, where inclement weather was common, it was no big deal. Ella was not so calm. She ran around in a frenzy, instructing my father to "buy some hextra food from di city." My mother was to "catch plenty watah inna di baat tub," and the gardener was to "board hup all di window dem and prepare di kerosene lanterns." My mother thought that it was quite unnecessary to board up all the windows, but she obeyed most of Ella's other orders. She did wonder why there was so much panic and preparation for just a little storm.

Well, Hurricane Charlie hit with a vengeance around ten o'clock that night. Immediately, the power went out, and there was darkness. Then the howling winds and lashing rain started and did not stop until early morning. My parents had been lying in bed, not quite believing the deafening noises the storm was making, when suddenly the windows of the bedroom blew open and glass and debris and rain went flying everywhere. Ella ran into the room, picked me up out of my crib, and dashed into the closet, sheltering me from any harm. My parents and brother quickly followed, and we spent the rest of the night huddled together in pitch darkness in the safety of this inner sanctum, me in the protective arms of Ella and the rest of my family crammed in wherever they could fit. At precisely two o'clock in the morning, Ella announced it was time for my feeding. As a practice, she had sneaked into my parents room every night at two o'clock to give me my bottle, whether I needed one or not, and this routine was not to be broken just because of a hurricane. The problem was, the milk and bottles were in the kitchen, so she sent my father on a life-threatening journey to the kitchen to get my bottle. At this stage, almost every window in the house had been blown in; glass was strewn in every room, rain continued to pour in, the wind was howling, and the mango tree that used to be in the front garden had crashed through one of the windows, and branches and leaves were blowing everywhere. I often wonder what gave my father the courage to make that journey. Was it the love he had for his beautiful baby daughter, or the fear of facing Ella's wrath if he disobeyed her orders? I think it was the latter, but miraculously, one hour later, my father arrived back in the closet with a bottle of milk, and I was woken for my feeding.

The morning light sent my mother into shock. The severity of the damage to the house was mind boggling, but she often told me that the most amazing sight was looking down the mountain at the few poorly built shacks that had survived and seeing right inside the houses. Almost every roof had been blown away. Few people in the village could afford a concrete house, so the damage to their homes was severe. Looking around the garden, all the beautiful flowers had disappeared, leaving behind a trail of bare branches, now all leaning sideways, blown over by the powerful wind.

Roads were in a terrible state. There was no electricity, no water, no phones, and no way of communicating with the rest of the world. After a few days of total isolation, my father, struck by a severe case of cabin fever, decided to venture down the hill to assess the damage and try to reconnect with civilization. Ella did not think this was a very good idea. At the best of times she referred to Kingston as "that wicked city" and never approved of a journey down the mountain unless absolutely necessary. Like many country people in Jamaica at the time, she had probably never visited Kingston in her life, but she had heard it was a "sinful" place and knew, especially after a hurricane, "much teeving han robbery is going to be happnin'."

My father ignored Ella's advice and started down the hill in his precious car that had miraculously survived unscathed. He found himself weaving his way around mudslides, boulders, fallen trees, and numerous other obstacles in the road, which made his journey painfully slow. He finally came within sight of Papine, the first little town at the base of the hill. All he had to do to complete this leg of the journey was to cross a narrow bridge over the river. As my father started to cross the bridge, he spotted a large boulder blocking the road. Parking the car he got out to determine if he could clear a pathway. He saw the water lapping over the bridge and could feel the current around his ankles but thought nothing of it. As he tried to figure out how to maneuver the boulder, he suddenly realized that the water was rapidly rising and the swollen river was about to break its banks. The water moved quickly up to his knees, and when he looked back at the car, his tires were already submerged, and the water had reached the doors. Dad ran to the car and leaned in the window to retrieve his keys and coat just as the car started to float away. He half ran and half swam off the bridge, jumping to safety on the river bank just in time to watch his precious car being swept away by the overpowering waters. The car quickly disappeared down the river, never to be seen again. Dad tried to catch his breath, not quite believing what had just happened; he was so relieved to have found safety and to be alive to tell the tale.

Dazed and frightened by the whole experience, Dad started the long journey back up the hill—on foot. He trudged up the mountain for hours, finally arriving home shortly after midnight, drenched and bruised from the experience. My mother and Ella, who had been worried sick about him for hours, were greatly relieved to see him walk through the door.

It would be another week before he ventured down the mountain again.

After Charlie, my parents, my mother especially, developed a new respect and fear for the word "hurricane." In fact, Mom would develop many new fears in the years to come. Hurricane Charlie was just the first.

CHAPTER 3

Letters back home . . .
"We're bringing Niamh home to die"

Life was not easy in the early years of colonial Jamaica, but my mother would never have complained about this, especially to me. I have deduced this from various old letters I found written to my grandparents. Some of these letters were from my mother, but there were also letters from the wife of my father's boss, who felt obliged, I am sure, to reassure my grandparents that their precious daughter was doing just fine. These letters were a wonderful source of information and gave me a little glimpse of what Mom's daily routine and social life were like back then.

My grandparents were always very worried about my mother in that "godforsaken place," and one of the letters I found attested to that fact. That particular letter was written by Helen, the boss's wife, who was very British and very colonial but seemed to have a warm heart. I know she thought she was laying my grandparents' fears to rest, however I doubt very much that the letter fulfilled its purpose.

One of the supposedly reassuring letters from Helen reads, "Your daughter and grandchildren are utterly adorable. We have all had such fun and laughter together. Maeve is so pretty, and she and Tom are so obviously in love with one another, that I just adore having them around. Of course, it would be nice to have your young people in Dublin with you, but Tom has a very good job, is thought the world of out here, and is, I am certain by his enthusiasm, doing very good work.

"We live an entirely different life in Jamaica—in many ways, it is a bad life—we have really nothing much to do. You almost have to hunt out your jobs to keep you busy. We live eleven miles from Kingston, and I find my husband is tired by the time he gets home from an exhausting day's work . . . Maeve tells me you worry a lot. Now, there is no need to. There are plenty of picture shows (no theaters though, except amateurs), crowds of visitors, picnics, and excursions on Sundays, etc., so we live a very good life . . . The food is quite delicious and plentiful—expensive, I will admit, but naturally, what you can't buy is always much better. The servants can be good, and they can be bad, but you get the same in England and I imagine in Dublin also. I really think the girl who does my washing and ironing works hard, and everything is done in the old-fashioned way. I have a mangle, and I got exasperated trying to show them how to use it. In order to iron, they have a most fascinating open pot in which they burn charcoal to heat the irons. One girl usually needs about five irons to keep them hot. Everyone has an electric iron, but to do the heavy household ironing, the servants prefer the old-fashioned ones.

"Transportation is the great nuisance. Very few people can afford two cars, and it means the wife has to go to town early in the morning with her husband and usually put in a day waiting for him to take her home. If you are on a bus route you can travel home in the slack periods. But life can be very pleasant; every afternoon we can have a good nap, not what you could do when you were teaching in Dublin.

"Now remember, do not worry. Worry won't do anybody any good, and it will only add years to your own life. If I can help you along with a letter about the young people, just don't hesitate. It is really almost as good as a visit from them sometimes when you hear from others about them. May I say how I do hope you yourself are coming into a fair and sunny path."

Like I said, I cannot see how this letter really eased my grandparents' fear, but the boss's wife really could write. I find it amazing how even this one letter exposes the contrasting feelings the British had, even in those days, in coping with day-to-day life in the tropics. As soon as you started complaining about the bad stuff, you immediately extolled the good stuff; it was as if you knew deep down that no one back in your rainy, cold, mother country would have the slightest sympathy for you about your lack of comforts. No matter what your tale of woe was, they could only visualize you lying on a beach under a palm tree, sipping a fruity rum drink in balmy 80-degree weather. There was a total lack of sympathy: "Oh, you got mugged? Oh dear, but I bet you were on a sunny beach when it happened, so stop complaining."

Looking back now, I can quite understand the love/hate relationship that Europeans had for their faraway colonial homelands, often finding themselves there through an unwitting set of circumstances and trying to make the best of it. The inconsistencies of emotions were quite understandable, because the hardships were real, but as soon as you recovered from some unpleasant experience, there was a new unique island adventure waiting for you around the corner, which always lifted your spirits. Like I have said before, such was life in the Caribbean.

Mom's letters to her parents were more personal and gave detailed accounts of life in our own little family. When I was nine months old, I got a bad case of whooping cough, which seemed to linger. I was in and out of the hospital, just like my mother, but I never seemed to get much better. I could not eat, and I lived on a diet of ice cream and soup, with Vitamin B shots every other day. These shots apparently traumatized me so much that even today I cannot handle injections without passing out. It is amazing how our lives can be dominated by events that we have no conscious memory of, but somehow, subconsciously affect us forever.

I do know my mother was very concerned about my health.

At two years old, I was still very sick, and my parents did not know quite what to do. I had been taken to every possible doctor in Jamaica, with no sign of recovery, so they decided to take me back to Ireland. My father, who was a very hard worker but not known for his great business skills, had surprisingly negotiated with his company to pay for the family's passage back to Ireland at least once every three years or whenever necessary. This was a huge bonus and enabled my parents to bring me home when they thought I was not going to make it to my third birthday.

My mother wrote to her parents: "Niamh [my name in Irish] is a terrible worry for us. I think the whooping cough left a terrible weakness in the poor darling." According to my melodramatic father, I was dying, and if I was going to die, "I would die at home in Ireland," not in a foreign land. So plans were made to head home.

This was my mother's first visit back home, and even though I would have thought it was under stressful circumstances, she was very excited about the trip, especially when she found out she would be traveling by plane to New York and from there on the luxury yacht, the *Mauritania,* to Cobh, a famous port on the southern coast of Ireland. "What do you think of that, Daddy? I can hardly believe it myself," she wrote, which made me wonder about her priorities. Maybe she knew deep down I was not really dying, so she could focus on the pampering she was going to get on her sail back home.

Cobh is a famous port because it is from there that most of the immigrant Irish families originally set sail from in the 1800s to their new homes in New York, Boston, and beyond. None of my direct ancestors made that life-altering sail, but judging by the hundreds of thousands of O'Briens in the United States today, I am sure I have distant cousins who did. My great-great-grandparents never left their homeland; they stayed and toughed it out.

Back then, many young people in Ireland never made it to adulthood; only the fittest survived, and thank goodness my father was one of the fittest. His mother had sixteen pregnancies, but only eight children lived to adulthood, my father was number seven. He had a brother who died from measles and another who died from an asthma attack, illnesses that would be curable and preventable today. Number-seven child was one of the healthiest people I have ever known. He was never sick a day in his life, that is, of course, if you don't count the time he had a stroke at sixty-nine, but that was inevitably self-inflicted, the result of years of nicotine abuse.

At two years old, I was showing no signs of being part of this healthy O'Brien gene pool. This was very unsettling to both my parents.

My mother wrote to my grandparents, "Thank you for all your prayers and offerings of Holy Communion for Niamh." Everyone was praying (at that time even my father still prayed) that my undiagnosed illness was caused by some mysterious tropical allergy and that as soon as I got back to Ireland, I would miraculously be cured. Whether you believe in prayer or not, it seemed miraculous because that is exactly what happened.

The great welcome home my family received at the dock in Cobh was heartwarming. After many hugs and tears, the aunts, uncles, and grandparents all headed off to a restaurant to sit and catch up. While they were all chatting at the table, they sort of lost track of me. I am sure this was only because of the excitement of the moment and not because they just forgot about their "dying" sick child. Anyway, I had climbed down and wondered over to another table where a man in a bright red robe was sitting. I am sure the bright red robe caught my attention, and I proceeded to climb up onto his lap, at which point I started picking up food off his plate and eating it with my fingers.

He was very gracious about the whole thing, but finally asked "Where are your parents?" as he was peering around the room trying to spot which negligent family was missing a child. He was looking to me for answers, but seeing how I was only two years old and not talking very much, I was of no help. Besides, I was busy eating solid food for the first time in over a year. When my parents finally noticed their little girl was missing, they panicked. Much to their relief, they eventually spotted me halfway across the restaurant at the stranger's table.

I had not chosen just any old stranger's lap to climb up on; I had chosen to befriend a cardinal no less! They approached the esteemed holy man's table with much embarrassment and profuse apologies, however, when they saw that I was actually eating his potatoes, they forgot about their embarrassment and became overjoyed with excitement. I was not going to die after all; their prayers had been answered (my melodramatic father's words again).

For the entire visit to Ireland, I was eating and getting well. This phenomenon only confirmed my grandfather's belief that my illness was caused from living in that hot, humid, mosquito-ridden, godforsaken place. So my parents, with great encouragement from my grandparents, decided to leave me in Ireland with my aunt Maureen while they returned to Jamaica with my brother. Over time, I have come to believe that the only reason they would do such a thing was because they really did not want to take any chances with my health.

It would be two years before my mother got back to Ireland to pick me up. You would think that this would have left me with all sorts of abandonment-syndrome problems. However, surprisingly, I only have fond memories of that time. I put this down to the fact that my wonderful aunt and uncle, who had no children of their own, packed a lifetime of love into those two years. I was their "precious gem," their "wee dote," and I could do no wrong. They put me up on a pedestal so high that you would get vertigo if you looked down.

My aunt Maureen, who is now in her nineties, still calls me once a week from Ireland to tell me how great I am. When she dies, I will no longer have anyone left in my life to tell me how great I am. I am very aware that she has a totally overinflated opinion of me, but I still love to hear it—wouldn't we all?

In the letters my mother wrote during those two years, she frequently asked about "darling Niamh." She sent me dresses and gifts, so I can assume my mother missed me. I don't have any memory of missing her, although I must have. I do know I missed my brother because my aunt tells me I used to walk around with my left hand clenched all the time. When she asked me why I did that, I told her I was holding my brother in there. I might be in denial, but I promise you I really do not have any resentment or noticeable scars from being left by my parents in Ireland for two years. I truly do believe it was a very positive and nurturing experience.

CHAPTER 4

Do you believe in miracles?

Meanwhile, back in Jamaica, my mother was meeting new friends and discovering a new social life that I am sure she found quite bewildering. My parents had moved down from the mountains of Irish Town and were renting a house in a centrally located residential district of Kingston off Hope Road. They rented one of the five houses on a large property owned by the Fisher family.

One of Mom's letters back home to her parents read, "Mr. Fisher is Jamaican, and his wife is English. They fight all the time. Mrs. Clark, in another house, is separated from her husband and has several boyfriends. She is English, and her husband, a nice man, left her a month ago. He was brought up a Catholic but lost his religion a long time ago. Another woman who is from Dublin, married an Englishman, left him years ago, and is now living with some other man, and she is a grandmother! I have met so many people like that that I could go on forever. Most of them are nice people and see no wrong in what they are doing. Do you remember Mr. Duffy? I told you his daughter is out here. Well I just heard the other day that she is a divorcee and that he is a big shot in the Free Mason's lodge here. You live and learn. This island is going to hell."

Maybe my nanny Ella knew what she was talking about when she referred to Kingston as "That wicked sinful city"!

You must remember that my mother came from a family of very conservative, albeit dysfunctional, staunch Catholics. Divorce was not an option for an Irish Catholic at that time. No matter how miserable you were, you stuck it out, and, as I have said before, you went to the pub to drown your sorrows and forget about it.

I am not so naïve to think that no one in Ireland ever had affairs, but they were always well hidden, never spoken about, and certainly never flaunted in public. So when my mother found herself living on a 1950s version of *Wisteria Lane* or, for you older readers, a 1950s version of *Peyton Place*, I am sure she found it all quite shocking and was not sure what to make of it. The tone in the last sentence of her letter about the island "going to hell" does seem to convey an uncharacteristic touch of anger, so maybe she was beginning to have moments of doubt about her own marriage surviving this island's den of iniquity—premonitions she should have paid more attention to.

I did not seem to miss much during the two years I was left in Ireland. My parents' social circle was rapidly growing, even though, according to Mom's letters, they were living very economically. "Our only luxuries are the pictures or dinner parties or the occasional picnic. We went to a dinner at some people's called Phillips recently. They are white Jamaicans, very nice people with a lovely home and a huge station wagon. They gave us a scrumptious dinner and took us to the pictures afterward. I met some people the other day called the Hockys. He is working for the British Council attached to the library here. We had them and their little girl up for dinner. They took Peter to Morgan's Harbour today for a swim. A couple of weeks ago we went on a launch that belongs to Carl Abraham to a little island called Lime Cay just off the coast. We brought our own lunch, beer, and Cokes for Peter. It was very hot on the island, and we all got sunburned. A friend, Bill Radburn, brought his underwater fishing gear with a gun that floats and a snorkel and flippers for feet, so Tom had a go at that but said the fish were too quick for him. Peter had great fun with their little girl. I enjoyed it very much, but the sun was really killing. We are all peeling after it."

My mother seemed to be enjoying her life in Jamaica, although at the beginning, her social life was somewhat limited to mostly expats and white Jamaicans, which was to be expected, I suppose. Her life generally seemed to be relaxing and comfortable. Her curious health problems were still not diagnosed, so during those early years she did write about having weak spells that prompted short stays in the hospital every now and then. She would always seem to recover over time. The one thing my mother never did was complain about feeling sick. She would just go and rest when she needed to, with no fuss or bother.

However, I am sure my mother's illness and bouts of weakness were not helping my parents' relationship. My father had gotten used to such a fast pace of life that he had a hard time slowing down. He had bundles of energy, and she had none. He hated hospitals and would get squeamish around them, so he spent as little time there as possible. Slowly, my parents started spending fewer hours together. But even if my mother had some doubts, deep down, about the stability of their marriage, I am sure she brushed them aside quickly. She was still so in love that he thought the good times would never end.

Four years had passed since my mother first landed on the hot shores of Jamaica. I am not sure exactly when my father started cheating on her, but I have deduced it was around that period.

I say this because it was at that point my father made a huge decision that rapidly added to the polarization of their relationship. What happened was he fell madly in love with golf. Not a problem in and of itself, but his problem was that he chose to join the most social golf club with the most popular bar in Kingston. Golf was a sport my mother despised and consequently was never invited to partake in his outings. What started out as an occasional game on Sundays, gradually became two or three games each weekend, and the occasional drink at the club after work slowly became a regular habit. This change in lifestyle can be destructive to any marriage, but I believe in Jamaica it can be fatal. The most popular bars always have beautiful, young, single women hanging around waiting to pounce on the young, single guys. This is a common mating ritual performed in countries all over the world. I have often witnessed it. However, the problem in Jamaica is that the majority of the single women don't wait for the single men; they have absolutely no hesitation in hitting on married men, young or old, as well. There seems to be a total disregard for the fact that they are spoken for and therefore off limits. To a weak man, this temptation can be too much to resist, and believe me, when it came to resisting women, my father was a very weak man.

Tom playing his beloved golf circa 1958

Mom continued on, even though she must have started to notice a difference in my father. Maybe it was so gradual that she felt she had no need for worry. She wisely stayed socially active and soon developed a warm circle of girlfriends. She became especially close to a wonderful English lady called Imelda. In her letters to her parents, she wrote, "I went to hospital to see my friend Imelda yesterday. Poor woman, as soon as she went into hospital, some Jamaican girl started to run off with her husband. He is completely infatuated with this girl who is much younger than he is. Imelda is thinking of leaving him. However, it is none of my business. They have no morals here!"

Mom was definitely aware of all the infidelities going on all around her, but I am sure she never thought it would happen to her. However, knowing what I know now, and looking back at the gradually increasing comments in her letters about Tom getting busier and busier, I can tell that his cheating had already started. Every letter during this time seemed to end with some version of "Tom is working truly hard, poor dear," or "He even has to go in on Sundays and I am fed up." In another letter, "P.S. Tom busy at work" When he decided he was not going to make the journey back to Ireland with my mother to pick me up, she should have seen a red flag, but instead she wrote, "He works terribly hard, and it is all for the good that Peter and I will be at home among my family for a few months, and he can devote all his time to work. Last night he came home at eleven o'clock after being down in the country all day."

I wish I could put myself in a time machine and leap back to 1955. I would jump up and down in front of my mother and scream, *"No! No! No! Can't you see what is happening? Don't be so naïve. He is not in the country, more like in the country club. And he is not working until eleven o'clock; he is with some Jamaican girl until eleven o'clock—a girl who is much younger and who he is infatuated with."*

Hindsight is a frustrating thing. Back in 1955, my mother was either in total denial or completely blind.

The voyage back to Ireland to pick me up and bring me home seemed to take a terrible toll on Mom's health. She arrived in Dublin very weak, and the entire family knew something was seriously wrong. Doctors were called in, but none could determine what was causing this inexplicable weakness and inability to eat. In fact, some of the doctors were saying it was all in her mind and that was nothing physically wrong at all. My poor mother must have been very frustrated at this suggestion; she knew something within her body was not working right, but what?

Even though I was only four, I have vivid memories of the family all huddled around my mother's bed, fussing over her and praying the rosary every day. I knew something was wrong, but my aunt Maureen and Mammy Daly and Daddy Daly (as my grandparents were called) did a good job of keeping my brother and me distracted enough to prevent us from worrying. Mom got worse and worse, and one day I remember hearing the sirens of an ambulance pulling up to my grandparents' house. I got quite alarmed by the noise and the confusing events that took place as they rushed Mom out of the house and put her in the ambulance. But once again, the loving attention my brother and I got from our aunt and grandparents gave us a sense of security and comfort that somehow melted our fears. Surprisingly, my father was not called. I am not quite sure why, but I am guessing it was because my long-suffering mother thought it unnecessary. After all, he was "working" so hard, why bother him?

But the doctors in the hospital could not figure out what the problem was. My mother got weaker and weaker, and everyone thought she was slowly dying. Then, one day, the priest was summoned to give her the last rights, or as it is called today, "the anointing of the sick." This is the sacrament that Catholics receive when they are close to death to ease them into eternal life in peace. Not surprisingly, my mother went on to receive this sacrament several times in her life, but she always defied the odds. As soon as she saw the priest coming, she would hastily recover from her near-death experience as if to say, "I am not ready to die yet!."

The priest who came to administer the sacrament in this instance brought along a famous "miraculous" cross. He proceeded to bless my mother with the cross as he prayed. I remember being in the hospital room and looking up at the faces of my grandparents and my aunt, sensing something good happening.

I don't fully understand the power of miracles or how they work. I do believe there is a higher source of power or energy that exists beyond human limits. It is common sense to me. You only have to look around you to know that we humans could not have created life, our world, or our universe. Most people call this higher source of power *God*. My Catholic family sure did; not only did they have great faith in God, they believed in the power of this miraculous cross. Maybe miracles occur because of the unwavering belief that what you are praying for at the time will happen. Failure is not an option, so you "will" it to happen. At those intense moments of meditation and prayer, we somehow are able to tap into a higher energy field, to tap into God, and so things beyond normal human abilities occur. That is what I believe faith to be, and they say faith can move mountains and cure sick people.

However, what happened next is not so easily explained, because the "miracle" did not come from anyone who had been praying at my mother's bedside or from my mother herself. It came from outside the room. There was a knock at the door, and a doctor walked in with a bottle of cortisone in his hand, announcing, "I would like to try one last thing." Luck would have it (or miracles would have it?), he had been reading an article about a fairly new illness called Addison's disease, and many of the symptoms my mother had seemed to match. Addison's disease occurs when your adrenal glands stop working. This causes a domino effect of dysfunctions within the body, the main one being that the body does not produce adrenaline, so a desperate weakness overtakes you. Within one day of receiving the cortisone, my mother started to feel better.

Was this a miracle? My mother and grandparents certainly thought so. Their faith was only strengthened by what had happened. The most important thing was that there was finally a diagnosis, and there was a treatment that would allow my mother to live a normal life. All she had to do was take her cortisone and get enough rest each day, and life would be very manageable. Hooray! No more doctors telling her it was all in her mind and insinuating she was a hypochondriac. How relieved she must have been. In fact, the entire family must have been greatly relieved to finally know the cause. Mom slowly regained her strength, invigorated by her newfound cure, and she planned her return to Jamaica, this time with both her children in tow.

Maeve on a trip to Ireland with her sister Maureen

CHAPTER 5

Life in Red Hills . . . best friends, bats, scorpions and black widow spiders

Soon after my mother returned with me to Jamaica, Dad revealed he had accumulated enough money to buy a house. I found out later he actually borrowed the down payment from my Daddy Daly, something my mother quickly reminded him of whenever she needed ammunition.

He found a wonderful place in an area called Red Hills. There were large deposits of bauxite in the soil there, which made it look red, hence, the name. Our new three-bedroom house was built entirely of reinforced concrete blocks with a layer of smooth cement covering the outer surface. Most houses in Jamaica were built this way, supposedly to withstand earthquakes. The house was painted a bright, sunny yellow; it had a flat roof, so there was no chance of it blowing off if or when another hurricane should strike. It had a large, open veranda that swept around the entire back of the house and led up to the edge of a huge L-shaped swimming pool. From the veranda, the 270-degree views of the city and mountains were spectacular. The house was situated in the middle of three adjoining crescent-shaped mountain ranges that encircled the valley of Kingston and its shores beyond. To the south, it was as if the entire city lay at our feet. In the distance, the activity of the ships in Kingston Harbor and the outer blue Caribbean Sea added to the ever-changing panorama. To the east and west, the mountains dominated the scene. It felt as if the hills were embracing us, even though they were miles away. Our expansive garden was thick with tropical vegetation, and many varieties of fruit trees and plants grew uninhibited. In anyone's mind, the house was set in perfect paradise. But as we all know, a house does not a home make.

As luck would have it, the next-door neighbor to our beautiful hillside house was an English lady named Gina. Gina had married a good-looking black Jamaican during World War II while he was stationed in England. His name was Victor Beek. Victor was a pilot in the Royal Air Force and flew planes and helicopters. In the 1940s, a mixed-race marriage in England was very rare and often unacceptable. Consequently, the couple faced many prejudices living there, the worst of which was total rejection by her family. In fact, she told me that if her sister saw her and her husband walking down the street, the sister would cross the street so as not to have to talk or even make eye contact. That was very painful for both Gina and Victor, I am sure. So they decided to move back to Jamaica where their lives were easier and mixed-race marriages were quite common. My mother immediately made friends with "Auntie Gina," who also had two young children, Dudley and Rosanna, the exact same ages as my brother and I. Back home in Ireland, my mother's friendship with Gina would have been unlikely as Gina was a British Protestant and my mother an Irish Catholic. But in Jamaica, they were far away from their cultural homelands, and contrary to what they had been taught as young girls growing up, these differences became totally unimportant. What was important was they remained the closest of friends for the rest of their lives.

Gina's husband lived a very similar lifestyle to that of my father. Neither of them was home much at night. They never seemed to get past the college phase of life where partying and drinking and womanizing was the norm. Maybe it was because they had never gone to college and always felt robbed of those experiences. Maybe it was because they had both gotten their teenage girlfriends pregnant and were forced into marriage at too young an age. Whatever the reason, my mother and Gina found themselves with a lot in common: far away from their homeland, both with two young children, and both stuck in marriages that had many painful challenges. The common bond they shared forged a very strong friendship.

"Your mother was like my twin sister," Gina often told me. To my mother, Gina was not only a friend; she was a confidant, a mentor, and a therapist too. Who needs therapy when you have a close friend? The strength Gina and my mother gave to each other helped them survive the many hard times to come. Unlike my mother, Gina was never indoctrinated by the Catholic Church. She was not taught that divorce was never an option no matter what, and consequently, she was not quite as long suffering as my mother. She had a much more confrontational and volatile relationship with her husband.

The "twins" Maeve and Gina 1966

My mother and Gina seemed to empower each other, and the one thing that kept them going was their great sense of humor. They often told me stories of the mischief they got into, but one tale in particular stands out in my mind. It occurred one night as my mother and Gina were sitting on our veranda looking down on the lights of the city of Kingston. Knowing their husbands were having a good time somewhere out there without them, Gina suddenly jumped up. "Let's go find them!" she suggested to her friend.

I think just enough whiskey had been consumed to give them the courage to do this, so they got dressed up, jewelry and all, jumped in Gina's car, and set out to locate their wayward husbands. My father could usually be found at the bar at the local golf club, playing pool and buying everyone drinks, especially attractive young women. Victor, Gina's husband, was usually at the Officer's Club, and like Dad, springing for drinks and trying to impress the pretty girls who were not allowed into the club but were always hanging around outside with the junior-ranked men.

The Officer's Club was the first stop. My mother and Gina pulled into the parking lot, nervously giggling a bit but full of determination. They got out of the car and strolled straight through the crowd of young girls, brazenly pushing open the door of the Officer's Club. Jaws dropped and bodies froze. You could have cut the air with a knife it was so tense, and the two women casually walked up to the bar and plopped on to stools, puffing on their cigarettes and blowing smoke into the air the entire time. Not only was the Officer's Club considered a sacred men-only zone, but women were never allowed to sit at the bar. The extra pleasure of knowing that every man in the club knew exactly who Gina was and had a good idea of why she was there felt sweetly revengeful. The other husbands were probably panicking, thinking all the officer's wives had somehow had a meeting, and their wives would be the next to walk through the door. But for now, the stares were on Victor as his fellow officers held their breaths and waited for the fireworks to start.

"Two whiskeys, straight up with a dash of water," Gina demanded. To everyone's shock, the bartender obliged, I guess he was so embarrassed he did not know what else to do.

Victor quietly came over, trying not to look angry, and asked them in a soft voice, "What are you two doing here?"

Gina responded loudly "We have come to party!"

"Please don't make a scene" he begged her.

The wives were loving it. For a few brief moments they had all the power. The confrontation with Victor was a bit anticlimactic, and after that, they sat quietly and finished their drinks, no man daring to question their presence. But their mission had been accomplished; there was no need for further embarrassment. When they got up from the bar to leave, Victor sheepishly followed them outside. He drove home behind them in a very subdued mood, knowing his friends would heckle him about that night for a very long time. When my father heard about the incident the next day, he was greatly relieved that the women never ventured to the golf club, and he actually spent his nights at home for a few weeks just in case my mother had any plans of repeating the escapade.

Birthday party in Red Hills Niamh, Peter, Rosanna, Dudley and friends circa 1958

For the most part, I enjoyed my growing-up years in Red Hills. The strain the marriage was under at that time must have been heartbreaking for my mother, but she kept her problems hidden from my brother and me and held the family together as best she could. Although I often noticed my father's absence, he always turned up eventually, and the appearance of a family life was upheld.

My mother's goal was for our childhood to be as fun and interesting as possible. She always planned fabulous birthday parties and always went overboard to make our friends feel welcome. We had a pool, so that was always fun, but we had no television, so evenings would be spent playing cards and a variety of board games. Scrabble was a favorite but, being Catholic, we had learned to play poker and black jack at an early age, thanks to the many church bazaars and fund-raising events we attended.

Our father was the only family member with a car so when we were not at school, our days could get quite boring as we were stuck at home a lot. But my brother and I kept busy by taking long walks and going on neighborhood adventures. Many times my mother would accompany us on our walks, and we would encounter strange Rastafarians, often stoned spouting quotes from the Bible. We never felt in any way threatened by these odd characters, although I am sure they thought we were the odd ones. In those days, it was very safe to venture out.

One of our favorite places to explore was a nearby cave that was home to thousands of bats. My mother never had the endurance or the desire to climb up the steep hill side to the cave, so I am sure she had no idea it was full of bats. However, my brother and I found it fascinating, so along with our adventurous neighborhood friends, we decided to make the cave our secret clubhouse. We used to meet there regularly—just us and the bats. Many times, as we approached the entrance, hundreds of bats would wake up from their sleep and swarm over our heads, flying out the mouth of the cave in a panicked frenzy, not knowing if we were friend or foe. It's amazing we didn't get bitten or, worse yet, get rabies.

In fact, it's amazing we survived any of the various wildlife and insect encounters of our childhood—there were many. I used to sleep under a mosquito net, which gave me some sort of protection but not much. One night while I was sleeping, I woke up to feel a stinging on my neck. I was groggy and thought it felt like a strong bee sting and started to flick it away when I felt another hit in my thumb. Then I knew it was not a bee. I started screaming, and my Dad came running into the room thinking I was being murdered. When he turned on the lights we discovered about fifteen black scorpions climbing all over me. Thank goodness, he managed to flick them off without any more of them stinging me. Come to find out, there was a huge family of them living under my carpet, and during the night, some of them had crawled up the sheets and on to the bed and all over me. I did not seem to suffer any serious side effects from the stings. I was in luck, as they were black scorpions, not red ones that are the more dangerous kind, but the stings were still very painful. The gardener discovered the rest of the nest the next morning and proceeded to chop all the scorpions into little pieces with his machete right in front of my eyes. I think I was more traumatized from witnessing this violent massacre than I was from the poisonous stings. My mother would always shake out her sheets before going to bed after that. She also got into the habit of shaking out her shoes before putting them on, as they were a frequent hiding place for scorpions—a wise decision, as a scorpion would invariably fall out.

Another time, a black widow spider fell out of a tree and landed on my brother's face. Everyone was screaming at him, "Don't move, don't move, whatever you do, don't move." He stood there terrified, not knowing what to do.

Mom yelled, "Flick it off, flick it off!" Of course, she made no attempts help him do this, as she was just as panicked as he was. He was on his own, standing there, just frozen with fear. It clung to his cheek for a few minutes, eventually biting him, and then he flicked it off in a hurry. A very painful experience, but he got over it.

There was always the assumption that if you lived in the tropics, you had parasitic worms of some type. So every three months, we got a dose of worm medicine, whether we needed it or not. Of course, pesky mosquitoes were always around, but they were not too much of a problem until an outbreak of dengue fever or malaria caused everyone to go on high alert. The one thing we did not have to worry about was snakes. Jamaica had no snakes, and unlike Ireland, it was not St. Patrick who ran them out, it was the mongoose. Some wise landowner had introduced the mongoose to the island during the slave days, so that the workers would not have to worry about being bitten as they chopped through the thick cane fields. Lucky for us, the mongooses apparently ate every snake.

However, even without snakes, there were enough menacing and highly poisonous insects to always be on the lookout for. Strangely, my mother never seemed too perturbed by these dangerous creatures. After all, we were in the tropics, and we had to learn to deal with them. All except flying cockroaches, of course—even though they were the harmless ones. Unless we had streaks of poison running up a leg and the leg was turning blue (which actually happened to me one day), we were never taken to a doctor. I guess my mom had had her fill of doctors. I never did find out what creature had bitten me to cause the poisonous streaks up my leg, but sometimes ignorance is bliss.

We not only had the various insects to worry about, and of course, the occasional hurricane (although none was as bad as Charlie), we also had to deal with earthquakes. We experienced many while living up at Red Hills. At least once a year there was some kind of earthquake, and some were quite severe. They were nerve-racking, because, unlike a hurricane, you have no warning an earthquake is coming. As soon as we felt the ground shaking under us, Mom would rush us to the veranda doorway, and we would stand there huddled under the frame until the shaking stopped. She always thought we were magically safe there. Our house was built of solid concrete so, luckily, the only damages we suffered from an earthquake were cracks in the walls. But still, Mom would get very anxious whenever an earthquake occurred. She did not like them. During an earthquake, you have no control over anything that is going on, and for those few seconds, it can be terrorizing. You just have to wait for the shaking to stop and pray the building will not start falling down around you. You are at the complete mercy of nature. The results are unpredictable, and even though our house always remained intact, we never knew which one might be "the big one." Fortunately, we never did experience "the big one," so to my mother, they were just another added adventure of living on the rocky mountainside of Red Hills.

CHAPTER 6

It's hell to be poor

The Addison's disease that had inflicted itself upon my mother's fragile body was, for the most part, manageable. The major problem she had was lack of energy, and she learned early on that a couple of hours rest in the afternoon helped her live a fairly normal life. I have no idea how John F. Kennedy coped with the Addison's disease that he suffered from during his demanding presidency, but he did, and so did my mother. I know it was not easy for her to sleep during the hot afternoon hours, and I remember seeing her frequently awaken in a pool of sweat with wringing wet clothes.

One day, Dad announced he was buying a window-unit air conditioner for their bedroom. I thought my mother was going to explode from happiness. It was the most precious thing you could own at the time. She was practically jumping up and down with excitement the day Dad arrived home with the magical cooling contraption. After he installed it, she did not leave her room for three days. In fact, my brother and I used to sneak into their room and huddle in there as often as we could, just to feel that wonderful cool breeze. This truly helped Mom cope with her life-saving rest every afternoon.

The three or so hours of sleep Mom needed each day were critical, but as young children, we really did not realize it. We would frequently interrupt her attempted nap, bursting through the door with some trivial question or piece of information. This prompted her to put a sign on the door that read "Do not wake me unless the house is on fire!" That sign stayed up for quite a while.

So we got the message. Except, one day, the house really *was* on fire! The lady who ironed for us liked to use the old-fashioned coal irons as she had always done. Those irons would be placed on top of a cast-iron dish of burning hot coals. On one particular day, the cast-iron dish was placed too close to the curtains, and somehow the curtains caught on fire. Then the flames from the curtains caught the mahogany dresser on fire, and that caught the bedclothes on fire, and soon the entire room was engulfed in flames. When my brother and I saw the flames shooting from the room, we ran to our mother's door and started pounding on it.

She shouted back, "I told you children not to wake me unless the house was on fire!"

"Well, guess what, Mom!"

Fortunately, most houses in Jamaica were made of concrete, and ours was no exception, so the walls and roof could not burn. The fire was pretty much contained to the furniture in that one room. The gardener stuck the hose through the window, and everyone frantically got buckets of water; the inferno was soon put out. But for Mom and for us young children, it was another exciting day in Red Hills. That evening, when things were fairly back to normal, the sign on my mother's bedroom door came down. I am sure she was racking her brains to think of a new sign to put up that would help keep us at bay during her quiet time. But she gave up. This was Jamaica after all; anything was possible, so why bother?

During the school year, my brother and I were never back at Red Hills before evening. At this stage, my mother still had no car, so we had to wait for my father to pick us up, usually after work, which was often quite late. This did not bother me at all. I thoroughly loved school. I soaked up everything I could get out of it, every sport and extra-curricular activity I could find. I used to work hard and always got good grades, so I was very amused when I came across a letter my mother had written to her father informing him that "Peter is very clever. I never have to worry about his schoolwork. Niamh is not as clever, but she has other qualities that make up for it." What! Lucky thing I found this letter when I was already an adult.

I was on the honor roll every year, so I could not have been that dumb. I think she was just comparing me to my genius brother, and although I hate to admit it, he really is much smarter.

I went to an all-girls Catholic school, Immaculate Conception High School, run by a Franciscan order of predominantly American nuns and some well-educated Jamaican nuns. It was not just a high school, because it actually started in kindergarten and went through A-levels, which is an advanced two-year, post–high school course. Our tough curriculum was based on the British system of education, with our exams written and graded in England. I attended Immaculate for nine years and completed my A-levels there.

As I grew up in Jamaica, I was exposed to a culture that was unlike anything my mother had experienced in her own childhood. Ireland in the 1920s, '30s, and '40s had a population that was 99.9 percent white. I, on the other hand, had classmates and friends that were a mix of many races: Chinese, Indian, Hispanic, black, white, and all shades of brown. Amazingly, I never felt different. We were all of the same upper-middle-class socioeconomic level, and we were all getting a very thorough education, thanks to the nuns and the Cambridge-set exams we had to pass. Consequently, we were equals socially, and we all got along well, which leads me to believe that most of the prejudices in the world are not racial at all, but social.

When you live every day with people you have a lot in common with, you forget what they look like on the outside and only see their behavior. If they behave and talk just like you, you can't help but relate to them. I remember going on a school field trip one weekend to the beach. About twenty five girls—our entire class—were all sunbathing and having a good time. An American tourist walked by us and stopped. He stared at us for some time, amazed by our diversity, and asked us if we were a group from the United Nations. We were a bit perplexed by his question, but when we looked around at one another, we could see why he thought that. It had just never occurred to us how diverse we were.

Even at a young age, however, I was very much aware that the majority of the population of Jamaica was black and extremely poor. I was white, and although not wealthy, I had a much higher standard of living than 90 percent of the population. Mom was very aware of her socially privileged position and started volunteering to work with the poor when I was a small child. She taught me a sense of social responsibility that would stay with me my entire life. As it is called today, Mom was a "stay-at-home mother." She never earned a paycheck while in Jamaica and never held a position of authority in the workforce in her life, but she found her calling with the poor. She had a powerful influence on the lives of many underprivileged people. And just as she did with her own children, she always had a way of making them feel important, special, and worthy of a better life. I guess the fulfillment she got from this work balanced out a lot of what was lacking in her marriage. The gratitude and appreciation she constantly received from strangers filled the void and empowered her to keep going.

Maeve (second from right) and volunteers, always working for the poor

Poverty really was, and still is, pervasive in Jamaica. I have a friend who, in 1967, at eighteen years of age, decided that he was going to live among the poorest of the poor in the ghetto of Kingston to see if he could help them in any way. He wanted to put himself in their shoes, at least for a short while, and learn what life was like for those desperately needy people. For any privileged person in Jamaica who had even the tiniest conscience, it was almost impossible not to want to do something for the less fortunate, because poverty was so rampant, but my friend went to an extreme, in my opinion. The neighborhood he chose to live in was Trench Town (yes, the same Trench Town that Bob Marley sings about), and life there was hell. My friend was either very brave or very stupid, I'm not sure which, but in the six months he lived in Trench Town, he had the most terrifying but eye-opening experiences of his life. Here is an excerpt from his story.

The population of Trench Town was 99.9 [percent] black. I cannot remember seeing a white or Chinese or Indian person during my months of living there. This created a firm belief (supported by the reality of the situation) that only black people were the real poor in Jamaica. Anger toward the whites (of which I was considered one) ran very high. During my first two weeks, no one said a word to me. Not a word! In effect, I did not exist. For about the second two weeks, almost every man and boy (never women or girls) threw all manner of verbal abuse at me, the most common being, "What you doin' here, Buoy, yu is a communist?" I never answered or showed any visible response—though I was mostly scared shitless during this time. Toward the end of the first month, the tone and questions changed. People began to ask my name and why I was there.

In those days, West Kingston crime was individual, random, and based mostly on passion. While I am sure there were collections of "rude boys," the criminal gangs, and in particular, the political criminal gangs, had not yet begun to operate. Major crimes were mostly emotional and violent in nature: rapes, stabbings, beatings, etc. They tended to be an excessively angry reaction to some perceived disrespect or violation.

My most violent personal experience was under a street lamp, about seven thirty one night, where about five of us were gathered. We never heard the shot, but one of the group fell to the ground with half of his throat blown away. The four of us remaining turned on our heels and raced wildly in separate directions. I figured it out later that none of us knew who the shot was really meant for; it could have been any of us, as life in Trench Town in those days was super cheap, and about twenty dollars could get anyone killed.

Another incident was seeing the police chase a man through the West Indies Pulp and Paper depot that I managed, shooting at him as he ran. Mortally wounded, the man finally collapsed into the concrete gully at the back and died. Also on that very same property, a man came in and chopped another man's hand off with a machete—the latter had taken away the former's woman.

People felt relatively safe within their particular tenement yard, seeing it as a fort or castle of sort; there were high zinc fences, and many topped were with barbed wire. Rooms were small, and everything was in one room. The size and comfort of the bed was important, and entire families slept together on the same bed. Everyone had a "hot plate" to be used for cooking, and frying was the most common way to cook the bully beef or occasional fish. More commonly, a meal was hot sweet tea, hard-dough bread, and some processed cheese.

The daily routine for everyone included a "fresh"—a shower at the standpipe in the open common area of the tenement yard. People would remain in their underwear and lather all over. The soap was usually Carbolic or Lifebuoy, and the distinctive aroma could be smelled for a long way. Most of the day was spent lounging around, talking and playing dominoes with the radios on competing stations RJR and JBC, turned up to full volume. In the evening, everyone bolted doors and closed every window within an hour or so of sunset. Self-imposed lockdown was a way of improving safety. Only criminals, rude-boys, and prostitutes walked Tobias Street after nine o'clock, and you did not want to encounter any of them.

When people went out, they almost always were accompanied by friends. I do not recall walking anywhere by myself. Maybe we did not intellectualize it, but at a primal level, the message was clear: "My friends protect me and define me; see how bad I am?" My paseros (whose names I do not recall) were all large and very mean looking.

Yes, it was hell to be poor in Jamaica and still is hell—as it is in any country in the world. To this day, I never take for granted that "there but for the grace of God, go I." I am fortunate to have the family I was born into, dysfunctional as it is. At least my parents gave me opportunity, education, and enough love and support to get me through life, for the most part, unscathed. I am always grateful to Mom for teaching me to look outside of my own little circle to see the rest of the world and figure out how to make a difference. She used to say that even if we can only change one person's life for the better, it is worth it.

My mother knew that the social structure of the poorer classes in Jamaica was complicated, but it always seemed to be the women who carried the heaviest burdens and were the most vulnerable, so it was the women she tried to help the most. Among the indigent in Jamaica, family life was nonexistent as most men only stayed around long enough to impregnate their partners. Children often didn't know who their fathers were and, certainly in Kingston, were often neglected and left to roam the dangerous streets alone. The lack of a strong family unit forced these neglected children to find their identity and sense of belonging elsewhere. Unfortunately, most ended up in gangs that were only too happy to take in these lost children and teach them the criminal ways of street life. Jamaica, for the most part, was a matriarchal society. Grandmothers did their best to raise the children as the mothers worked hard to bring home a few dollars a day to keep the family fed. Boys did not have good male role models in their lives, so the cycle of irresponsible fatherhood was perpetuated generation after generation.

I never quite understood how this lifestyle came about until an educated Jamaican explained it to me. I was told that males have an inherit drive to have as many children as possible with as many partners as possible to ensure their genes will be passed on and procreation is guaranteed. Before monogamous societies were established, I guess that is how it used to be. In the days of slavery, this lifestyle was encouraged and rewarded so that the slave population would grow rapidly, much to its owner's delight. The more prolific a man was, the more prestige and status he had among his peers. This, of course, was a very satisfying lifestyle for most men, all the fun and none of the responsibility—so naturally, they tried to keep this tradition alive for as long as they could get away with it.

But it is a serious problem. I once met a man in Jamaica who had thirty-five children. How could you ever pull yourself out of poverty with thirty-five children! I asked him why so many, he literally told me, "I don't go to bat if I can't make runs." I began to understand why Jamaican men were the way they were, but it still upset me greatly to see women allow themselves be used in this manner, guaranteeing a perpetual life of hardship and poverty for themselves and their children, especially their daughters. After all, birth control was available, and marriage was a popular institution among the middle class.

Then one day, when I was about thirteen, I was with my mother, who teaching a class of adult literacy to approximately twenty very poor women. I asked one of the women how many children she had. She told me six, and I could tell she was destitute. I asked her how she managed to take care of six children. She told me that four more babies were living inside her, and all ten had to come out or else she was going to die.

Did I hear right? I asked her who told her this, and she said "the doctor." She was talking about the witch doctor (who, of course, was a man). The other women were nodding their heads in agreement. Mom and I were shocked at their ignorance. They did not even know how babies were made, and nothing the "white woman" could say was going to change their minds. Believe me, my mother tried. They got a little puzzled at my mother's attempt to clarify the truth, but they knew they dare not question what the witch doctor had taught them, because he could put a voodoo curse on them in a second. I am sure that poor, misguided woman went on to have her four more babies.

Shortly after the witch doctor conversation in class, I opened the front door one morning to go to school and saw three dead puppies hanging from the frame of the door. Blood was dripping everywhere; their little necks were twisted and broken. I screamed at the top of my lungs and started to shake with shock. A voodoo curse had been put on our family. When our cook and gardener heard the screams they came running. They saw the puppies and dropped to their knees, held their heads in their hands, rolled their eyes to heaven, and started to pray to God for mercy.

"Lad, mi Gad, wi goin' die," they kept wailing. They were as scared as I was. Dad came running and tried to console us by defusing the situation with humor, which he always did. I believe his comment was, "If it was an Irish curse, I would be worried, but it is only voodoo curse. No problem."

I wondered why anyone would want to do this to us. My family was well-known and respected among the poor who lived near us. Mom, and also Dad, had taught us to be kind and considerate to anyone who was less fortunate, and there were many. But word had got out that my mother had interfered and tried to change the beliefs and traditions that were sacred to the local women, and this was her punishment. Unlike both the cook and the gardener, my mother and I knew that the witch doctor could not actually put a terrible curse on us. But psychologically, it was an unnerving incident. It brought home to me quickly that outside of our safe circle of friends and family, we lived among people whose culture and superstitions were very different from ours. Even though I was born in this country and called "a white Jamaican," I was different. This new awareness caused me extreme uneasiness. I am sure it was a familiar feeling for my mother, but to me, it was the first time I felt so far out of my comfort zone.

CHAPTER 7

It's easy to fall in love
with Jamaica's majestic beauty

Taking weekend and holiday trips to explore Jamaica's most magnificent sites, of which there were many, was often used to help us forget disturbing events. These excursions, where we could just savor the natural beauty of the land, gave us great joy. Most of the time it was just my mom, my brother, and me and a couple of other families that would all pile in together and share a rented holiday house or a friends "country" house. Since my father seldom accompanied us (he was always "busy"), I would not exactly call these vacations memorable family-bonding moments; they were more in the category of survival escapism, especially for my mother. I can never recall having a strong urge to send my father a postcard that read "Having a wonderful time" or "Wish you were here," so, unlike Mom, I must not have missed his presence very much. However what made up for it was that we always had great fun with our friends, and so did she. My brother Peter and I would spend the days climbing coconut trees, swinging off ropes into deep blue lagoons, catching soldier crabs, or just roaming the beach. At night, we would play board games, have pillow fights, and get into as much mischief as we could get away with.

In fact, I recall one memorable vacation when I was about eleven. Mom and Auntie Gina had rented a house on Long Beach on Jamaica's North Coast.

One night, we heard drums beating for a long time quite near our house. The boys, Peter and Dudley, decided they would sneak out to see what was happening. They followed the sounds down the beach and through some bushes only to find themselves witnessing a local "Pocomania cult" meeting where everyone was dressed in white and wildly dancing around and around in a circle to the beat of the drums. A chicken was being sacrificed in the center of the circle, and blood was spewing everywhere.

The dancers slowly worked themselves into frenzy until they were in a hypnotic trance, wailing and moaning the entire time. We had always been told that Pocomania was an old African spiritual ritual that had been passed down through the generations and still occurs today. Peter and Dudley had never actually witnessed anything like it before. They were mesmerized as they peered through the shrubs.

All of a sudden, they heard a deep voice from behind them angrily shouting, "What you boys doin' here?" One of the cult members had discovered them.

It scared the daylights out of Peter and Dudley. They jumped up and took off running as fast as their legs would carry them. They admitted to us girls later that they were terrified that they were going to be scooped up to replace the chicken as some kind of human sacrifice for the ritual. There were no more attempts to sneak out of the house at night again— at least not on that trip.

Dudley and Rosanna Beek with Niamh on vacation Circa 1961

Such stories added excitement and a sense of adventure for the younger group, and the adults enjoyed these vacation breaks just as much as the kids did, if not more.

After keeping half an eye on us kids during the day, Mom and her friends would break out the cards in the evening. Poker was her favorite game, and it was accompanied by many whiskeys, straight up with a dash of water. The husbands who had joined their families would fish during the day and play dominoes all night.

When Dad accompanied us, which was a rare occasion in my recollection, he would golf during the day, but at night he turned to poker and dominoes, which he was very good at. The men's drink of choice was good old Jamaican rum or a cold Red Stripe beer. Although the accommodations were usually a bit rustic (we could never afford to stay in a hotel), we were always immersed in lush tropical vegetation and surrounded by crystal blue waters and pristine beaches. These were glorious settings that, as young children, we just took for granted.

From the days when Christopher Columbus's stories were first documented, up until today, visitors and locals alike have been enjoying the spectacular beauty of this sun-drenched island. In his journals back to the king of Spain, Christopher Columbus wrote, "The banks of the rivers are embellished with lofty palm trees, whose shade gives a delicious freshness to the air, and the birds and the flowers are uncommon and beautiful. I was so delighted with the scene that I had almost come to the resolution of staying here for the remainder of my days." I know my father shared Christopher Columbus's sentiments. He certainly wanted to stay there for the remainder of his days. He was madly in love with this beautiful "land of wood and water."

Dunns River Falls in 1966

Our vacations would vary between the mountains on some occasions and the beaches on others. These were the days before full-blown tourism, when places like famous Dunn's River Falls could be enjoyed just as it was. Like those in the Blue Mountains, the falls were natural explosions of water bursting from the side of the mountain, cascading downward over large boulders until finally crashing into the sea. There were no cement retaining walls or manmade steps, nor concrete parking lots. No human chains of tourists gingerly navigation up the falls hand in hand. It was raw and rugged and a magnificent display of nature's force in all its glory. We were spoilt by many such places on this paradise island. Even though Mom had only a fraction of the stamina Dad had, she was always a trooper on these holidays and made huge efforts to keep up with us. I do not recall her ever reaching the very top of Dunn's River Falls, but she always tried.

One weekend, Mom and some of her friends decided to rent a beach house in a coastal town called Saint Ann. There were four families in total. We all piled into our cars and set off on our adventure across the winding mountains to the North Coast. On the way, we stopped at a beach called Puerto Seco. It was not the best beach in Jamaica by far, but the attraction there was the water slides. I am not exactly sure how high the tallest slide was, but I do know it held exactly twenty-five people on its steps. The reason I know this was because Mom, not to be outdone by her young children and all their friends, decided she was going to have a turn. The climb up was easy, as I was ahead of her. I reached the top and flew down into the water below. What a thrill. As I was swimming back around to the bottom of the steps to take another exhilarating ride, I began to notice that nobody on the steps of the ladder was moving.

I looked up to the top of the slide to see Mom frozen in place with a terrified look on her face. I yelled up, "You can do it, Mom," and all my friends started yelling, "You can do it." The twenty-five strangers waiting in line behind her were copying us in a low chant: "You can do it, Mom." She was like a statue. The chant began to get louder, "You can do it, Mom. Just close your eyes." Soon the chant became a yell, and they were all shouting, "Just do it, damn it, and hurry up."

It was no use, the courage she had mustered for climbing up the ladder had completely petered out at the top. As I started excusing myself to the people at the foot of the ladder for making them step off, everyone suddenly realized they were going to have to go backward down the ladder to let this crazy woman off. I apologized to all twenty-five disgruntled people in turn as they slowly dismounted. Peter was given the job of climbing up the steps to retrieve Mom, who timidly started the backward decent once she had the security of her son behind her.

It was amusing but, at the same time, discomforting to witness my mother's fear. Even though I was not yet twelve, I never thought Mom was afraid of anything, except cockroaches. I had only ever observed fierce courage in how she dealt with the overwhelming challenges life had thrown at her, but I guess I would allow her to be human this once.

When we got to our rented house, she made herself a whiskey, straight up with a dash of water, to recover from her day.

Peter O'Brien and Dudley Beek on a camping trip circa 1964

CHAPTER 8

I hate family secrets and this is a big one

I am not sure if Mom did the right thing by trying to keep up the appearance of a normal marriage with most of her friends and family. But that was what she chose to do. I am not of the opinion that parents should dump their problems on their children, even their adult children, but one thing that really bothers me is family secrets. I do not believe in keeping family secrets, especially from the family itself and especially secrets that will inevitably come to light at some stage.

Having said this, you can imagine how enraged I was when I found out that a huge family secret had been kept from me for twenty-two years. Dad sat me down one day, and with embarrassment in his voice, he told me I had a half sister named Bridget. She was twenty-two and had been living in New York with her mother and stepfather most of her life. He showed me her photo, and she was beautiful. She had big, blue, sultry eyes, dark hair, and flawless sun tanned skin. No question that she was his daughter, and I was about to meet her for the first time.

Apparently, Mom had known about Bridget even before she was born, but my father had asked her not to tell me. He claimed he was afraid of losing my respect and love. Peter had found out about her when he was about twenty-two. He was sworn to secrecy also. I was angry, very angry. Not at the news that I had a new-found sister—that was rather exciting—but at the fact that my parents had kept me in the dark for all those years. Even with all his flaws, I loved my father; I would always love him. Did he not know that? He should have been worried about losing my mother's love and respect (which I am sure was questioned many times) but not mine. Most of the time it was easy being his daughter, but you had to be a saint to be his wife. Even so, having been kept unaware of my half sister until I was thirty-two years old left me with a sense of betrayal, a feeling that I have not fully gotten over even today.

By a quick calculation, I figured I was between eight and nine when this illicit affair took place. No wonder Dad seldom joined our mini vacations and was rarely home for dinner. He was obviously much occupied elsewhere. As a married woman now, I can only imagine what heartache this relationship must have caused my mother. In her gracious way, she never shared the painful details with me, but in later years, I did hear a lot about it from Auntie Gina.

The frequent betrayals my father caused over the years were difficult enough to bear, but they were always short lived, with no emotional attachment. For him it was only about the chase.

I am sure psychiatrists nowadays could put a label on this behavior, sex addiction or maybe love addiction, or maybe it was just because beautiful women constantly threw themselves at him, and his ego could not resist them. I don't know why, but he was just one of those individuals who confuse sex and love. I think there are a lot of people out there like that, and they are always causing great pain to their spouses. However, with Dad, after each conquest he came back to my mother with his charming witty ways, and she always took him back. This time, however, there had been real complications—a baby. Dad would be entwined in the mother's life forever. This was a life-changing moment for Mom. Truth be told, according to Auntie Gina, my mother was consumed with jealousy at the thought of the possibility of losing her husband to another woman, and she had every right to be enraged. But only Auntie Gina heard her rants and sobs. Later, Mom told me that she had wept—a lot.

Gina was the perfect friend to have at a time like this, because she had gone through similar betrayals. In fact, I remember my mother telling me a story when I was much older about Auntie Gina getting into such a jealous rage one night when she found out her husband was with his girlfriend that she got into her car, drove to the girlfriend's house, and rammed her car straight through the closed gates, crashing it into the side of the house. Sounds a bit crazy now, but I know it made Auntie Gina feel vindicated in some dysfunctional way. In fact, knowing Auntie Gina, she probably looked at her wrecked car the next day and thought, *It was worth it just to see the shocked look on that cheating SOB's face.*

I am sort of glad Mom did not share her fury with her children at the time. What good would it have done to expose us to all the turmoil she was going through? After all, we were still very young. I think every woman who has ever faced this kind of betrayal in her marriage has to deal with it in her own way. I am sure my mother wanted to beat the hell out of Dad and then pack up and go back to Ireland. I know I would have, but that is not the path she chose. After the anger settled down, and I assume a commitment was obtained from my father to stay in the marriage, she decided the best thing for her and her children was to stick it out. The fact was, I believe she was still obsessively in love with Dad and did not want to lose him.

In a calculated scheme though, I am sure encouraged by Auntie Gina, my mother begged Dad to adopt Bridget into our family when she was born. Wow, to have come up with that solution she must have been extremely panicked at even the remote possibility that my father might start a new family with another woman in which case she would lose him forever. A bit of a desperate move in my opinion, however, the sad thing is that Mom truly loved my father, and I believe she was the only woman he truly loved too— but they just couldn't get their act together. Each time he repented for his wicked ways, she believed he would change, but he never did.

The problem was that my father had conveniently omitted to tell Molly, Bridget's mother, that he was still married with a family when their relationship was going on. So, needless to say, it was quite a shock for her to find out that Maeve existed, much less that she wanted to adopt her daughter. Molly did not agree to the adoption and the affair soon ended. A couple of years later, she married a very loving man and moved to New York. Dad remained supportive to his other daughter his entire life, but that was his nature. Later, when Bridget came into my life, Mom and I grew to love her very much. It was difficult not to, as she had inherited my father's outrageous charm and Irish wit.

No wonder Mom had many a whisky, straight up with a dash of water. She had a lot to deal with. As I mentioned before, no woman enters marriage with the intention of being blindsided down the road by an unfaithful husband, but sadly, it happens. The fact that she decided to stay in a marriage that was very painful, and I am sure, at times, humiliating, was ultimately her choice, even though it was not an easy one.

I believe one of the ways she learned to cope with her distress was to distract herself through her tireless work with the poor. Another reason she could manage, I believe, was because she had so many supportive close friends. And she was always a loyal friend back. She used to come to the rescue of any friend who was in trouble and needed her help. She became a champion fighter, especially for women who were trapped in an abusive or unbearable relationship. I guess she could relate to what they were going through. I am not implying that my father was ever physically abusive—especially to my mother—quite the opposite, but you could say his frequent betrayals were great emotional abuse.

One of the special friends my mother rescued from a very painful marriage was an English lady named June.

June and her husband had arrived in Jamaica from England in the 1960s. They were a typical expat family with two small children. June was a gentle lady, and she and my mother became very close friends. After a few years of living in Jamaica, as often happened, June's husband started having an affair with an attractive young black Jamaican girl. He was always with her, but again, very typically, he did not want to leave his wife or give up his marriage. He wanted his cake, and he wanted to eat it too. However his long-suffering wife was very distraught at the whole situation and was trying desperately to figure out a way to escape her unfaithful marriage. My mother started plotting, first teaching June how to save her airfare from the grocery allowance, (a trick Auntie Gina had taught her) and then how to plan the getaway before her husband could blink. They knew if he ever got wind of the fact she was planning to leave, he would never allow it. He would cut off all her finances, watch her every move, and make her escape pretty much impossible. They had to be sneaky.

When June had finally saved the one-way airfare for her and her two children, they bought the tickets and started secretly planning for the day of departure. When that morning arrived, the children got dressed in their uniforms as if it were a typical school day. No suspicions could be aroused. As soon as her husband left for work, my mother arrived to pick June and the kids up, and she drove them straight to the airport. They boarded the plane and never returned to Jamaica. What a freedom fighter my mother had become!

When June's husband arrived home from work, Mom immediately got a call from him. "Where are June and the kids?" he asked.

"They have gone home to June's parents' house in London," Mom proudly told him.

Maybe today, people would say June was kidnapping, but it's not like he didn't know exactly where his children were. Fact was, it did not seem to matter very much at all, because shortly after June went to England, the girlfriend moved in and June and her husband got a divorce. So I guess my mother had done the right thing. June never forgot what her friend Maeve had done for her, and later on in my mother's life, this became very important. It's amazing how feverishly she fought for June and others to leave their bad relationships, but up to this point, she had never tried to disentangle herself from her own.

My beautiful sister Bridget with Dad and Maeve 1987

CHAPTER 9

Nicotine, a very addictive drug

Although there were many whiskeys, straight up with a dash of water, throughout the years, my mother was certainly not addicted to alcohol; she just enjoyed drinking socially or on the many stressful occasions she had to endure. However, she was addicted to nicotine. She was born in an era where the movies of Hollywood made smoking look glamorous and sexy. Like a majority of people born in the 1930s and '40s Mom smoked from a very young age. This activity had a profound influence on me, so thanks to her, I have never smoked—as an adult that is.

I am told that when I was two and my brother was four, my mother gave both of us a cigarette and told us we had to smoke it all the way down to the butt. I guess she was using some sort of reverse psychology, which now would probably be considered child abuse, but back then, she thought of it as good parenting. Peter coughed, spluttered, and turned green. He never touched another cigarette in his life (of the legal kind, that is), but for me the experiment backfired. I loved it and smoked the entire cigarette to the butt and then asked for another. I smoked from age two to four. Whenever anyone placed a lit cigarette into an ashtray, I would pick it up and start smoking when they were not looking. There are photos of me actually puffing away, so although I have no recollection of it, I know it is true. How Mom was able to get me to give up cigarettes at four, I have no idea, but I did. I hope nicotine gum was not involved, but when I was about twelve or thirteen, I witnessed an incident that made me know I would never take up the nasty habit again.

It was a hot, sunny day up in the mountains of Red Hills. I did not see Mom leave the house, I only saw her return. She walked in the door dripping in sweat, red in the face, and puffing and panting as if she was about to expire. She collapsed into a chair, and considering her normal low-energy levels, I got very worried.

"Where have you been; what has happened?" I asked, panicking over her state of exhaustion.

"I ran out of cigarettes, so I walked down the hill to the gas station to buy a pack." The three-mile journey back up the hill in the midday sun had nearly killed her, but Mom was determined to have her smoke, whatever the consequences. It took her the rest of the day to recover. A deep feeling of repulsion rose up inside me as I watched her sitting in that chair gasping to catch her breath, all because she had to have a stupid cigarette. I was angry at Hollywood, angry at the advertising companies, and angry at the cigarette companies. Funny that, over the years, the second-hand smoke and the nasty ashtrays never bothered me, but watching Mom's desperate cravings and panic attacks when she ran out of cigarettes made an indelible impression on my psyche. I vowed never allow to myself to become addicted to anything in my life, especially cigarettes. After all, I had already gotten them out of my system at age four.

Niamh smoking away circa 1954

Mom's cigarette habit remained with her for most of her life, and the need to feed it created many challenges. There were times when there were no cigarettes to be bought in Jamaica. Imports were often sporadic and at the whim of the government's control of foreign exchange. At these times, my mother would smoke cigars, and on rare desperate occasions she even rolled an illicit "Jamaica Gold" spliff, the ganja weed, marijuana, that used to grow wild in our garden. It grew wild in a lot of places in Jamaica and still does today.

After the smoking ban on airplanes was put into effect, whenever Mom had to fly, her stress level rose by the minute the closer it got to take-off time. On one occasion, she just could not make it through the eight-hour journey across the Atlantic without her nicotine fix, and she actually lit up a cigarette in the lavatory of the plane. Of course, the smoke alarm went off, lights flashed, and the flight attendants came banging on the door. I don't know how she thought no one would notice that she was in there sneaking a puff, but in her state of craving, I guess she thought the punishment was worth the crime. What was she thinking?

My brother Peter really did grow up to hate smoking, and as an adult, he would not allow anyone to smoke in his house, not even Mom and Dad. It was years later, on a visit to his house in Canada, when I witnessed a side of Mom I rarely saw and another over-the-top cigarette incident. Peter was getting married to his incredibly hospitable second wife, Lucie, who graciously invited the entire family to stay with them for the wedding. However, smoking was a problem. Every time they had to have a cigarette, my parents were whooshed outside. This irritated my mother immensely as it was cold outside, and she had to puff quickly before hypothermia threatened. At this time, public smoking was still quite socially acceptable (not like today, when smokers are kept at such a distance you would think they had some highly contagious disease). Up until now, no one had ever banned Mom from smoking in the house, but she begrudgingly obliged her son's rules.

The wedding was a great success, and we all got back to the house very late and a little drunk—some of us more drunk than others. Not mentioning any names, but lots of whiskeys, straight up with a dash of water, were consumed. Mom realized that we had the house to ourselves, as Peter had said he and Lucie were going to a hotel for the night, so she decided to continue the party. There were eight of her grandchildren and six adults present. We cranked up the music, and all the kids began to dance. In the midst of the loud party, Maeve proudly stood up to her full height of five feet, and in a very defiant tone, she shouted to everyone, "Let's break the rules! Let's smoke in the house!"

Breaking the rules? I had never known my mother to break the rules; this was a side of her I found intriguing. She immediately lit up a cigarette and gave it to my father and anyone else she could find who would take one, including some of the teenage grandchildren, who unfortunately at that stage, were already seasoned smokers. Everyone was giggling and puffing. and the music was blaring; smoke was filling up the room. All of a sudden, Peter came stomping down the stairs in his boxer shorts and T-shirt.

"What the hell are you all doing?" Everyone froze. He was supposed to be at the hotel. *What the hell was he doing here?*

Well, Mom got an earful that night from her son, especially about the evils of smoking, but she took it calmly in stride as she always did. The next day, we all had a good laugh over it, even Peter and Lucie. I was proud of Mom's attempt to stand up for herself and defy the rules, even though her rebellion lasted only one night and was fueled by whiskey.

It took Mom almost fifty years to find the inner strength to give up smoking. She simply announced on day, very nonchalantly, that she was never going to smoke again, and she never did. *Just like that. Cold turkey.* What will power, what courage she had to muster to finally break the strangle hold nicotine had on her. It could not have been easy. Years of habitual behavior were ingrained. Lighting up after a meal; a cigarette with every cup of coffee, with every drink, on the telephone, at parties, and in conversation. The sad thing was, I knew she could have done it many years earlier. The strength was always there, she just never tapped it.

I wish she had. She would have lived a much longer life.

CHAPTER 10

The weekend of freedom . . . . what a breakthrough

My recollection of disposable income in our family growing up was that there wasn't any. The only time this bothered me was when the Barbie doll came on the scene, and I desperately wanted one. I still remember the price—exactly $10.40, including shipping from the United States, and Mom really wanted to buy it for me. Of course, she did not have the money herself, so she sent me to my father. His answer was, "No, we cannot afford it." I was devastated. I seldom asked for toys of any kind, so why couldn't I get Barbie? I felt complete and utter frustration; after all, all my friends had one. I know now how Mom must have felt being totally at the mercy of my father for every last penny. Dad could be a very generous man, but when it came to my mother, he deliberately kept tight control of the flow of money in and out of our house, which included a doll for me. This, of course, kept her totally dependent on him, and with his wayward lifestyle, it suited him just fine. After all, he had to make sure there was enough left from the budget for his outgoing expenses on wine, women, and song, or more accurately, rum, women, and reggae.

This was a side of their marriage that is very painful for me to look back at today. It was obvious how much he manipulated my mother by controlling all the finances. I suppose she accepted it because that's how life was in Jamaica at the time. It was very common for the husband to be the only breadwinner, and among her friends, very few wives worked. Certainly in the expats' circle, the husband was always the one who had been offered the job in the foreign land, and the wife had just followed along. As in a lot of marriages, money played a huge role in who had the power, and instead of keeping it in balance, in my parent's marriage, it was very lopsided.

Fortunately, however, Mom was aware she was being manipulated, and although she did not want to rock the boat and had been raised to be very tolerant, she was learning she did not have to accept this, and she started learning new tricks to compensate for her financial prison.

In spite of Dad's tight budget controls, meals at our house were always plentiful and varied. That is, until one year in the early '60s. Peter and I started to notice that something was different at dinner time. At least twice a week, the main and only course was baked beans and toast. Then it became three times a week, and soon beans and toast became the norm for dinner, and lunch became peanut butter and jelly, and breakfast was always eggs and toast. We began to question, where was the cereal and the ham and cheese; where was the ice cream; where was the beef? Mom was always vague when questioned about this change in diet, but in Jamaica, we were used to shortages, so we accepted our fate and never thought much more about it. This meal pattern went on for a year.

Then one day, Mom and Auntie Gina sat us down and announced, "We are going to Miami on a shopping spree."

"You're what?" Peter and I were shocked. Mom had rarely traveled without my father and that was only back to Ireland to visit the family.

"Auntie Gina has taught me how to save," she proudly announced.

"We've bought our tickets, we have the money, and we are going."

Dad, of course, thought the whole thing quite extravagant, but what could he do now? Mom had become independently wealthy from beans and toast, sneakily saving a little bit of the household budget each week for months. Surprisingly, I was not upset that this method of saving had sentenced me to a gaseous diet for such an extended period of time; I was just amazed at Mom's ability to save so much money, and that she could actually afford a trip with her best friend to America. Mind you, Miami was only about 480 miles away from Jamaica, but still, it was *America*. Maeve O'Brien had broken free from having to get her husband's permission for everything and was finally doing something for herself. Her first attempt at financial independence was not a huge step, but she was on her way.

Mom's trip to Miami with Auntie Gina was exciting. They stayed in a nice hotel by themselves and shopped and relaxed during the day, and I am sure had many whiskeys, straight up with a dash of water, at night. They walked up and down Flagler Street, thoroughly enjoying the wide variety of choices in clothes and shops, which of course were totally unavailable in Jamaica. They were in shopping heaven. Now, when I say "shopping heaven," I do not mean they went on a Paris Hilton kind of shopping spree; it was more like what I imagine a Whoopi Goldberg shopping spree to be like, not extravagant, just practical and fun. Mom brought home only four outfits, but one of them was for *me*. I still remember the cute red, white, and blue swimsuit with a frill skirt. Anything from America was exotic, so I was thrilled.

The shopping spree, known as "the weekend of freedom," was so successful that Mom adopted this method of saving on a regular basis. However, she did it so subtly and gradually that neither Peter and I nor my father ever really noticed any significant change in our diet, and so far, we have not been diagnosed with any residual deficiencies in our nutritional development. In fact, Peter and I both grew up to be very healthy, so our diet must have been adequate.

We really never knew how much she had been saving each week until she would just announce every now and then that she was going to buy a new piece of furniture, a new dress, or new shoes, and she did so without having to ask her husband for permission. Wow, what a sense of freedom this must have given her. Auntie Gina had done a good job of teaching her friend how to save, and my mother remained a very practical saver until the day she died.

It was not until 1963, when my mother received a small inheritance from her father, that she broke free of the financial stranglehold that marriage had bestowed on her. She immediately bought herself a car with the money. I will never forget it—it was a cute, yellow Volkswagen beetle we called "Bugsy." To Mom, Bugsy was better than a Rolls Royce, giving her her own transportation for the first time; this was a huge turning point in her life. The VW was a symbol of a newfound freedom she had been yearning for for a long time. No more relying on my father to take her places. In her generous spirit, she also spent some of the inheritance on the house, bought presents for Peter and me, and, of course, saved the rest. I was too old for Barbie then, but I know if I had still wanted the overrated skinny doll, she would have bought one for me in a heartbeat. Much to Dad's dismay, with the purchase of Bugsy, she managed to wiggle out a little more from under his subtle control. She now had wings and could fly. There was no turning back.

I was on the verge of becoming a teenager at this point, so to me, the car also meant a new source of freedom. Mom was much more available to take me places than my father ever was, so as long as my mother had the energy, she would happily drive us anywhere we wanted. *What joy!* Teenage years looked promising indeed.

CHAPTER 11

It's time for burglar bars

By the time I *did* become a teenager, Jamaica had gained independence from England and was well on the way to total self-government. The people had developed a deep sense of national pride, and Jamaicans of all color were struggling to find their own identity. In the '60s, the country was led by Sir Alexander Bustamante, a great leader, in my humble opinion, who had been championing the working-class cause since 1944. His philosophy and the philosophy of the Jamaica Labor Party, which he led, was to improve the standard of living and reduce social and economic inequality of the "little" man through a capitalist market economy, a win-win situation, I think, for all classes. As a result, Jamaica had remarkable economic growth during the '60s. In fact, some claim a 225 percent increase in the standard of living during that time. Statistics showed significant improvement in opportunity, education, and social services for the working class, in my opinion, finally sending the country in the right direction.

My life, however, was mostly unaffected by these changes except for the fact that the forward momentum Jamaica was experiencing seemed to lift everyone's mood. The white ruling British may have left the country, but things were much the same for me. My teachers had always been black and were still black, my doctor was black, my dentist was black, and people in authority who I grew up respecting were black; so what was the big deal about "Black Power" that kept filtering down from the United States? From my observation, we already had Black Power in Jamaica—almost everyone in power was black.

I remember when Dad made a business trip to Miami in the '60s. He had to ride a bus one day, and in doing so, he proceeded to take a seat in the back where he preferred to sit. The driver told him he could not sit there. Dad, ever the stubborn Irishman, was quite comfortable in the back of the bus, so he remained seated. The driver then informed him that the back of the bus was where black people sat; whites should be up front. Dad was in shock. He had never heard of such nonsense, and he refused to budge. The scene got ugly, and it ended up with my father being arrested for refusing to move to the front of the bus. What a mess America was. No such segregation existed in Jamaica, people could sit anywhere they wanted to on a bus; the only difficulty was finding a seat among the many chickens and overflowing market baskets.

Jamaica never had signs that read Whites Only. No Jim Crow laws were passed to consciously separate people of different races or religions. The big struggle the country faced was enduring the transition from years of British Colonial economic rule (which, by its very structure, made its conquered citizens feel inferior) to an era of economic independence (which, by its very structure, should elevate a country's confidence and pride). A newfound self-worth should emanate from a newly independent country. No more feelings of inferiority or suppression by the white rulers; the future was full of hope. Having complete control over one's own destiny was hugely empowering, and all Jamaicans, especially black Jamaicans, started to enjoy this newfound identity with dignity.

Although this is not an easy transition for any country, I believe that if Jamaica had stayed on the path that Bustamante was leading it down, one of a free-market economy, the transition would have been much more successful and produced much less violence, and my mother's and her entire family's lives would not have been turned upside down. But, unfortunately, this was not to be.

The changes in the mood of the country were gradual and crept up on us slowly. There had always been a few incidents of theft over the years while I was growing up, but they were mostly harmless high jinks that had more humor in them than fear. For example, the man who tended our garden, James, was a dear old soul but had a bit of a problem with the drink. He was always stealing our rum, but he would very cleverly refill the bottle with water, hoping my parents wouldn't notice the missing alcohol. My brother learned this trick from him, and it came in handy during his teenage years. One time, a close friend of my mother's had a fully cooked Christmas ham stolen from her, but she found out who took it and went to the thief's house and stole it back. This comical petty theft was gradually about to change.

It was around 1965 that Dad decided to install burglar bars on all the windows of our house. This decision was a result of an event that took place during a visit from one of my wild and crazy cousins from Ireland, Sheila, and her three flight-attendant girlfriends. They all worked for Aer Lingus, the Irish airlines, and they had each accumulated one month's vacation time. Sheila decided it would be exciting to spend their holiday in sunny Jamaica with her very hospitable Aunt Maeve. My mother was thrilled, of course, to have a rare visit from a family member from Ireland, so she went overboard to make sure the girls had fun. And fun they had, all except for one small incident. Sheila still retells the stories to her now-grown children of the wild antics that went on during that holiday.

Although Sheila was in her twenties at the time, I was only fifteen during this visit, so I was not allowed to partake in many of the activities. But I do remember the parties we had at home, and the stories of the crazy dates Mom had lined up for the girls.

Upon hearing that the visit from her niece and friends was imminent, Mom, unbeknownst to my father, went on a quick recruiting mission to the local golf club to find some prospective dates, which she felt would make the girls' vacation more fun. My mother had no shame, especially when doing something for her family.

Sure enough, she met a good-looking young man and his two equally good-looking friends sitting at the bar. They all seemed to have escort potential—at least they were single—so she told them about her niece and the friends coming from Ireland. She asked the young men if they were interested in attending a get-acquainted party at our house the following week. Luckily, the guys turned out to be really nice and not axe murderers (as my father had predicted when he found out what my mother had done). They became very obliging dates for the fun-loving Irish girls. Night after night, the group went dancing and drinking until the wee hours of the morning. The poor young men, of course, had to get up and go to work the next day, while the girls slept their hangovers, but somehow the diligent dates always arrived at the house at eight o'clock to pick them up for yet another night of nonstop carousing. I remember hearing comments about the development of dark circles and puffiness and slight stoops as the lack of sleep combined with alcohol consumption took its toll on these poor, unsuspecting men, But Mom was proud of her matchmaking handiwork and wasn't bothered that the lads were aging rapidly. If they did not have the stamina to keep up with her niece, that was their problem. All she cared about was that the girls were having a great time in Jamaica and that it was all because of her.

One of the young suitors owned a sporty, two-seater, red convertible in which he arrived each night to take my cousin down the hill to the "party," also known as the "wicked" city of Kingston. The other guys had their own means of transportation, but only the red sports car sticks in my mind.

Cousin Sheila on her visit to Jamaica 1966

After one of the nights of wild antics, Mom sat down with Sheila and her friends at the lunch table the next day (they never woke up before noon) to find out how the night had gone. Sheila announced it was great until they almost got arrested by the police at the bottom of the hill.

I thought my mother was going to gag on her coffee. *What?* Well, for whatever reason, they had all piled into the red convertible for the ride home. The problem was, this car was built for two, and there were five of them, so some were sitting on the hood and some were hanging onto the trunk. To make matters worse, they were all singing at the top of their lungs, and it was four o'clock in the morning. The police were charging the gang with overloading a vehicle, disturbing the peace, and driving drunk. Today, they would have been thrown in jail in a heartbeat, but this was 1965 Jamaica. Sheila, observing the look of worry on my mother's face, announced in newly acquired Jamaican fashion, "No problem, mon." No need to worry about a thing. Not only had Sheila given the police fictitious names, she had told them they were all with the diplomatic corps and could not be arrested because of diplomatic immunity. The police actually bought it. They let them off the hook with the promise to take a taxi the rest of the way home.

One week later, while we were all out shopping, we came home late one afternoon to find the doors of the house wide open and every room ransacked. The housekeeper had left for the day but claimed later that she had locked up the house before she went home. When we began checking our belongings, all the cash that our guests from Ireland had left in the house was missing, along with jewelry and various other items. This was the first time we had had an actual burglary, and it was not a good feeling.

Mom was embarrassed and shocked, and she immediately called the police. Lo and behold, who should turn up but the same local policemen who had attempted to arrest the group the week before. They actually were quite amused by the coincidence, and it was obvious they were not going to press charges for past transgressions. However, after declaring the burglary as likely an inside job and stating that there was nothing else they could do, they proceeded to get quite chummy with Shelia and her friends. I think they were remembering what party animals the girls were and hoped to cash in on some of the action. It was when the sergeant announced he would not turn down rum and water if it was offered to them, that my mother graciously but quickly whooshed them out the door.

After the departure of the *friendly* police, it slowly sank into our minds that a stranger, maybe even a violent stranger, had been wandering around our house, rummaging through our things and helping himelf to our possessions while we were out. I began to feel quite sick and scared and vulnerable, feelings that would become all too familiar in the years to come. That was the night my father announced he was going to get burglar bars installed on all the windows.

A year or two later, my brother's motorcycle was stolen. Not from the garage mind you but from inside the house. Much to my mother's disapproval, and even though it used to drip oil all over the place, Peter had convinced her to let him keep his precious motorcycle in the living room. After all, you would think that should have been a safe enough place. Not so, however. One morning Peter woke up to discover his pride and joy had vanished. The patio doors were wide open and leading from the vacant spot where his 'baby" used to sleep, was a path of oil, revealing the route the thief had taken. The thief had quietly pushed the bike from the house up the driveway to the road where he must have eventually roared down the hill. My father had neglected to put burglar bars on the doors, only supposedly secure locks. Well, obviously, the locks were not secure at all, and this prompted my father to add wrought-iron grilled doors in front of every exterior door of the house.

Even though this was only the 1960s, when lesser crimes took place, it had begun.

Although these offenses were all forced intrusions, no one was injured. They were almost misdemeanors compared to what we were to face in the '70s and '80s. During these years, the race to keep one step ahead of the criminals got progressively more challenging, and burglar bars and wrought-iron grills began showing up on houses all over Kingston.

The grills were not enough to protect our family against the ever-increasing home invasions that became more terrorizing as the years went by. The criminals got more and more aggressive and physically violent, and it became almost impossible to avoid becoming a victim of some heinous crime or having a friend who had been raped or murdered. The challenge to keep safe was difficult. It was a monumentally stressful challenge—one which we would eventually lose, but not without a fight and not without experiencing a lot of personal sorrow.

But for now we were still in the safe '60s. Peter had even miraculously recovered his precious motorcycle. I am not sure how exactly, except I believe he got a lead from a friend that it had been spotted somewhere. After that, he slept with the bike beside his bed every night. I seem to recall he used to sleep with one arm resting on his bike as if in an embrace. If anyone dared to try to steal it again, it would not happen without a fight.

Meanwhile, I was growing up very quickly. I have always thought that being warm all the time and not having to be wrapped up in tight layers of clothes helps the body grow faster. I have no medical evidence to prove this; it's just an observation. Maybe it's because the body does not have to expend energy to keep warm and can use that energy to grow. Maybe it's because when the climate is warm, you're outside all of the time, and you keep physically active. You are in the fresh air climbing trees, swimming, and running—always active. For whatever reason, unlike most of my cousins in cold Ireland, I was fully physically developed at eleven years old. My body looked like it does now except there were no wrinkles or saggy parts. I had matured quickly, not only physically but also emotionally.

One of the reasons I was forced to grow up quickly was because I started high school at ten, due to a series of circumstances. Under the British system of education, which we had in Jamaica, high school lasted for five years. At the end of the fifth year, you could either head off to an American or British university or you could complete an extra two years of advanced classes and take another set of exams called A-levels (advanced levels). All in all, if you completed seven years of high school and passed all your exams, you had received a darn good education, and that is what I did. The end result was graduating from high school at fifteen—pretty young even for Jamaica. The two extra years meant I was ready to join the work force at seventeen. At this stage, if you did not travel abroad to university, you became an apprentice to the profession of your choice, and I chose computer programming. So, at the ripe old age of seventeen, I was well on my way to being a highly paid COBOL computer programmer.

Wow, it is startling to realize that my professional career started in my teens. Was I robbed of my youth? I am not totally sure, but I truly don't think so. This was not twenty-first-century America, where women take their time growing up; this was the 1960s in the hot tropical island of Jamaica, and things were different. For one thing, one's social life was crammed with at least three times the activity of a normal social life. The grown-up parties our parents threw always included us. We had many opportunities to learn social graces early, and we learned how to converse with people of all ages—young and old. We were comfortable around adults.

Also, there was no legal drinking age in Jamaica. I don't know if this was a good thing or a bad thing, but I never knew one teenager who had a drinking problem. We did drink, some more than others, but we did not do it to feel grown-up, we just did it to be social. Being able to drink at any age made it no big deal. Another cultural practice that helped us mature early was that we were well-informed about what was going on in the rest of the world. Even though we lived in a third-world setting, our newspapers were full of world events, and everyone in our crowd read the newspapers. Also, there were the friendships we acquired with many international visitors that came from all corners of the globe. We met Americans, Canadians, Swedes, Germans, Italians, Venezuelans, Indians, Syrians, British, Chinese, and others who exposed us to the happenings in their countries, including who their leaders were and what their cultures were like. This information gave us a deeper knowledge into the politics and current events of most of the developed countries. It also gave us a unique tolerance for other cultures, sadly, knowledge I think few US teenagers even care about today. So although I was young in calendar years, my teenage years were so jammed packed with socially rewarding experiences, that I didn't feel deprived of anything, especially my youth. I had enough youth to fill three lifetimes!

The only thing I have ever wondered about is what would have happened if I had gone to university in America or Britain in 1966, like some of my close friends did. It was a scary time certainly in the United States. With all of the civil unrest and the Vietnam War, none of my friends had good experiences. Although my parents wouldn't have stopped me if I had wanted to go, they never encouraged me either. One of those close pals who went to Berkeley got so completely messed up on drugs and the hippie movement that she almost lost her life. Her parents had to go rescue her and bring her home. My friends of color experienced such demeaning prejudice that they were severely scarred afterward. Some of the boys got drafted to serve in Vietnam, a terrible war. All in all, the '60s were not a good time to be thrown into the chaotic culture of America, especially for someone like me, coming from a small island. Did I make the right decision not to go to a US university at that time? Mom certainly thought so.

What I do know for sure is my seven years of high school in Jamaica were some of the best years of my life, and I give my mother of the credit for that. She gave me the freedom and trust that allowed me to get out of the house and enjoy myself. I had many good friends and, consequently, a very active social life. Every time I left the house, Mom always put on a confident face and simply told me to have a good time.

I know now, especially after raising three teenagers, that the happy face was just a façade. Deep down, I am sure she was a nervous wreck. Not only did she have to worry about the normal problems of raising an adolescent girl, but in Jamaica, we also had to worry about safety at all times. I owned my own car at seventeen and drove myself everywhere. My being independent surely gave her even more cause for worry. I know she went through some very nerve-racking times, but she never showed it.

Dad was the total opposite. He was so overprotective that I was actually glad he was not around much in the evenings to monitor my comings and goings. It might have been because he was so untrustworthy himself that he assumed all young people were just like him. He was probably right about some of the boys, but I went out of my way to avoid boys who were like him.

Thank goodness Mom was smart enough to realize that. At times, she would even cover for me, saying I was asleep in my room when I was really out partying. She would sneak me back into the house at midnight, my Dad being none the wiser. Mom was cool, and all my friends loved her. They actually loved my Dad too, because he was so much fun to be around, but they did not have to put up with him as the ridiculously overprotective parental figure. To me, at the time, he was anything but cool.

Tony Nunes and William Plant sailing their beloved Flying Dutchman circa 1968

CHAPTER 12

Meeting my soul mate

Because, as they say in Jamaica, I was "force ripe," meaning I grew up quickly, it may not be surprising that I met the man I was going to marry at the tender age of fourteen. Tony was seventeen, and had just returned from boarding school in England; he was now was in law school, and he was a sailor. I immediately decided I wanted to learn how to sail too. Actually, I started dating one of his sailing buddies, Mickey Barton, whom I had met at a party, and it was Mickey who introduced me to Tony. Although it was not love at first sight, Tony won my heart very quickly. Despite the dating change, Tony, Mickey, and I remained such close friends that people dubbed us "The Three Musketeers."

Mom loved Mickey, he being the only one of my friends who ever invited her to go sailing. She accepted and bravely set off in his little fourteen-foot dingy one day, with Mickey at the helm. One thing I have learned about competitive sailing over the years is that you have to be a little crazy to love it. Most of the people who are sane and have tried it, never try it again. In fact, I have often been asked, "You guys do this for fun? You're crazy!"

For one thing, you always get soaked, burned, and bruised. You can easily get hit in the head with the boom and invariably get verbally abused by the skipper for some apparent incompetence. You are always at the mercy of the elements, whether it is rain, fog, howling winds, blazing sunshine, or a total lack of wind, at which point you just sit and drift. If you are lucky, you manage not to fall overboard, suffer from hypothermia, or get your lungs full of water. On top of everything else, many times you can end up back at the dock with blood flowing from some wound that you were totally unaware of until then. I guess my mother was too sane to enjoy competitive sailing. She knew after one exhausting, wet trip that the wild sport was not for her. But still, she appreciated the invitation from Mickey and the opportunity to try something new. She often spoke of how kind and thoughtful he was to her.

Mickey was the type of rare friend you could call at four in the morning and ask him to get you an aspirin; if the only aspirin he could find was forty miles away, he wouldn't hesitate or complain, he would just drive until he got it for you. Loyal, loving friends like that don't come along every day, and both Tony and I remained very close to him until the day he tragically died in a car crash at the young age of twenty-one. He was returning from a party in Port Antonio when he took a corner too fast, flipped, and was ejected. His car rolled over on top of him, crushing him instantly. As you can imagine, we were devastated. In fact I remember going into complete shock and trembling uncontrollably was when I heard the news that Mickey was dead. The party was at the home of a friend, Arnella Flynn, the daughter of Errol Flynn, the famous movie star from the '30s and '40s. Although her father had died many years prior, Arnella and her mother remained in Jamaica at their cattle ranch in Port Antonio. Ironically, Tony and I were also invited but Port Antonio was about one and a half hours from Red Hills, and Mom thought, very prudently, that it was too far to drive to a party all in one night, so I was not allowed to go. I will never forget Mickey asking me if he thought he should go without us; I told him of course he should go. I know if we had gone to the party, Tony would have been the one driving, and Mickey would still be alive today. We lost a wonderful friend that night, and at his funeral, my mother wept just as much as Tony and I did.

Surprisingly, not only my mother, but Dad quite liked Tony too, saying he "had potential." Dad also thought sailing was a great sport. In fact, he decided the whole family should join the Royal Jamaica Yacht Club and learn to sail. At that moment, my life changed forever. Unlike Mom, I became an avid sailor and learned a sport that has defined my entire life. To this day, I have a great love affair with the water, especially crystal-blue Caribbean water, and I go sailing at every opportunity I get.

I never owned a boat in Jamaica, and yet I sailed every weekend. However Tony did own a little seventeen-foot boat called a Flying Dutchman that he had bought with money his mother Beth had left him in her will. Unfortunately, Beth had died of cancer when Tony was ten years old. However, his father, Mike, had remarried a wonderful lady, Christine, and I know one of the many things that attracted me to Tony was the stable and loving family life he and his four siblings seemed to have. He was ambitious, competitive, reliable, and full of life, and I loved him. I think this is why Mom conspired to let me sneak out of the house sometimes when she thought my father was being too protective. She trusted Tony, and so did I.

Tom O'Brien & Mike Nunes sailing in 1980 (a.k.a The Colonel and the Clown)

CHAPTER 13

Guns, corruption, political gangs and racial turmoil

During the late '60s, every now and then a wave of political tension and unrest would burst through the country like a mini earthquake. Everyone felt the tremors, and we would get anxious for a while, but as long as lives were not being toppled, life continued somewhat routinely.

The violence, however, was definitely increasing and, along with it, unsettling feelings. My family began taking more safety precautions, keeping aware of our surroundings at all times. Mom and her friend Gina could no longer openly sit out on her veranda drinking their whiskies, straight up with a dash of water, looking out onto the lights of Kingston and wondering where their wayward husbands were. That was probably a good thing, as I am sure it was an exercise in utter frustration.

The ugly fact was that no one sat outside after dark; it made you far too vulnerable. Once the sun had set, we all remained locked behind the grilled doors, hoping the barriers would do their job of keeping potential intruders out and keeping us out of harm's way. At this time, most of the violence was confined to the impoverished ghettos of Kingston, where rival political gangs had existed for years. But now these politically aligned criminals had surreptitiously acquired semiautomatic weapons, and with that, the violence started to escalate sharply.

These rival gangs were building up garrison communities, dividing the ghetto neighborhoods into sections that were controlled by deeply opposing political parties: the Jamaica Labor Party or JLP and the Peoples National Party or PNP. Neither side dared trespass into the other's territory, and just in case anyone forgot the rules, each party would constantly intimidate the other with frequent displays of gun power and violent murders. No one, not even the police, dared venture into these areas. The guns these political ruffians acquired before the elections remained in their possession long after the elections were over, and they were used in criminal activity for years to come. Owning weapons, and being in a political gang, gave these urban thugs a sense of self-imposed importance and entitlement that would encourage corruption and political favoritism that still goes on today. In fact, crime escalated so rapidly in these garrison communities in Jamaica, that in 2005, sadly, this beautiful island had the unwanted reputation of having the highest homicide rate per capita in the world. The only difference today is that the neighborhoods are now controlled by drug lords.

Another disturbing scenario during the late '60s and the '70s was the unsettling rumor that some politicians were aligning themselves with underworld organized-crime figures. To make matters worse, almost confirming the rumors, some suspicious deaths of prominent political figures took place. Politicians had the reputation of being totally corrupt and not to be trusted, and the police were not much better.

Up to this point, one may not have liked anything going on in politics, but it would have never seemed possible that running for a political office would make you a threat or that you had a good chance of losing your life. One man, a good friend's uncle became such a victim. He was slated as a possible future prime minister, leading the conservative JLP. One night, while attending a political conference in Montego Bay, he "accidently" sleepwalked off the balcony of his hotel. He did not die immediately, and an emergency call went out to the army to fly over life-saving blood. Getting the call was Uncle Victor, Auntie Gina's husband. As Victor was about to take off with the precious blood, a senior officer approached the helicopter and told him his orders were to disengage and return to base. No blood would be flown to save his life. Victor announced that it was his duty to fly the blood there, and he proceeded to attempt a takeoff. At this point, he was physically pulled from of the helicopter and informed that he would be court-martialed if he disobeyed orders again. My friend's uncle died that night and never got the chance to run for prime minister. Again, it was only rumor, but everyone surmised he had not sleepwalked off any balcony.

Unbeknownst to us at the time, a new breed of far-left socialists had started their destructive march to take over the government. Always well-hidden behind a veil of confusion and rumors, they were there alright, causing rampant political corruption.

Neither my mother nor my father was involved in politics, so even though the growing political tension permeated the country, our lives went on without too much interruption. Oh sure, Mom started to be more safety conscious and would drive through town with the windows rolled up and the doors of the car locked, causing her almost to pass out from the heat on many occasions. But we had heard of stories of men with machetes chopping at arms through the windows of cars to get purses and other valuables, especially at stoplights, so heat exhaustion was a small price to pay for safety. At home, as soon as dusk approached, the doors of the house were locked tight, and no one ventured outside after dark.

Like Mom, I just didn't want to accept the fact that life was changing. The only unsettling incident I can remember experiencing as a teenager I sort of sloughed off as no big deal. I was walking down the beach one day with my friend Rosanna in beautiful Ocho Rios when a young man ran up beside us and grabbed me in the crotch. Spinning around quickly, we both started hurling the foulest bad words we knew at him in our best Jamaican accent. He was so shocked that "di white gal dem" could actually speak Jamaican patois, and even more than that, actually knew such strong Jamaican curse words, that he ran off down the beach in disbelief.

Maybe he thought we were unsuspecting tourists who might like their crotches grabbed by a good-looking young Jamaican black man. However, as soon as he realized we were Jamaican, he was no longer interested. Rosanna and I had a good laugh at our instinctive reaction and how we had successfully run the young man off. It did leave me a bit shaken, but strangely, I found it more comical than threatening.

Niamh and Tony at Prom circa 1966

CHAPTER 14

A secret to a happy life . . .
Marry the right person

When I graduated A-levels in 1968, computers were just beginning to take over the world, and fortunately, I got in on the ground floor. I began work as a computer programmer for IBM's largest rival in Jamaica, International Computers Limited or ICL. The job was very rewarding, and I loved it. I also had Tony, the wonderful boyfriend who "had potential." That year, my potential-filled boyfriend decided he was going to compete in the 1968 Olympics in Mexico, sailing his beloved Flying Dutchman. I did not actually go with him to Mexico but found the whole experience exhilarating and loved being part of his support team. Since that first Olympic experience, our family has had three generations participate in the Olympics: Mike (Tony's dad), Tony, and our son Sean, who participated in the Sydney Olympics of 2000. I knew I was in for an exciting ride when I first met Tony, and I have not been disappointed. I have always craved adventure, and I try to live life to the fullest (I guess I get that from my Dad), so it was no wonder I was attracted to this adventurous Olympian. However, it was after this trip to Mexico that I noticed the picture of me he had had on his dresser for a year was suddenly replaced by a picture of his precious Flying Dutchman. Oh well, at least I knew that my biggest competition in life was going to be a boat, not another woman. Although he never really fussed over me or pampered me with lots of attention, Tony was totally devoted to me, and this was a good sign. I don't remember telling myself I had to marry a man who I believed would never cheat on me, but the thought was probably deeply imbedded in my subconscious. I was attracted to his unwavering faithfulness, and in my mind, he was exactly what I needed. I was not used to being fussed over and pampered by the men in my life, certainly not my father, so I felt comfortable with Tony's somewhat nonintrusive style. All that mattered to me was that he was loyal, dependable, and trustworthy. In fact, when Tony proposed to me in 1970, I was so sure he was the right one that I immediately said yes, even though I knew I would always have to share him with his other mistresses—boats and sailing. They never made me jealous though; I loved them just as much as he did, and I knew that we would always have the sport in common. I would never be Olympic material like Tony, but I was good enough to compete, and I always had fun. In no way was he going to spend every weekend in a sport without me. A lesson learned from my mother's mistakes.

When I agreed to marry Tony, he was still a law student with a pitiful income. I had a good job, and I was in love. The fact that I supported him through law school became useful leverage through the years, as I often reminded him of said financial contribution. Again, a lesson I learned from my mother's mistakes.

I know Mom was quite pleased with my career choice and my choice in husbands, and, for a while at least, life was smooth sailing, no pun intended. Someone once told me that one of the main secrets to a happy life is choosing the right partner. Needless to say, this advice did not come from my mother. In fact, the only advice she ever gave me was "Never marry a sweet-talking Irishman." Tony was one-quarter Irish, one-quarter English, and one-half Jamaican of Spanish/Portuguese decent. I remember when we first met, and he was obviously trying to impress Mom with his cultural heritage; he proudly announced he was a close descendant of Oscar Wilde, the famous author, obviously his Irish connection. I guess this could have given Mom cause for worry as Oscar Wilde did live up to his name. But she figured Tony didn't have enough Irish blood for him to be ruled out as husband material. Besides, he certainly wasn't sweet talking. Tony became a great addition and was warmly welcomed into our family. Over the years, he proved to be a supportive son-in-law, and I know Mom loved him deeply. It is not that easy to find the right soul mate in life, but in Tony, I was so fortunate to have found mine.

CHAPTER 15

"I'm a grandmother . . . does that mean I'm old?"

Exactly one year after we were married, I gave birth to our first son, Michael. I was very proud of the fact that I had started out my adult life by not repeating two of the biggest errors in judgment Mom had made. First of all, I married a good man, and second of all, I was not pregnant when I got married. I was determined to learn from her mistakes, and so far so good. The timing of the birth could not have been better, because the day I had to stop work at eight and a half months pregnant was the day Tony was admitted to the bar (the law bar, that is). The day my paycheck stopped was the day his paycheck started. We did not plan it that way, but it just worked out.

Mom, on the other hand—although she was bursting at the seams with pride—was not so sure how she felt about being a grandmother at the young age of forty-two. Dad, only half jokingly, was going around complaining to everyone, "Who would want to sleep with a grandmother?," Even though this was all said in jest, Mom realized there was some validity in his question. The unsuspecting title of "grandmother" invoked an immediate wave of panic. As with many women, she asked herself, *Does this mean I am now old? I don't feel old. Does this mean I am no longer sexy? I still feel sexy. Has this title launched me into the 'mature older women' category against my will?* All understandable questions. Thankfully, today the word *grandmother* does not conjure up the image of a gray-haired old lady, wrapped in a shawl, rocking back and forth on the porch knitting. And even in the 1970s, that image was becoming a myth.

The one thing Mom never had to worry about was how attractive she was, especially to men. Barely a day went by without her receiving some kind of compliment about how beautiful she was. I once heard a man meeting her for the first time tell her, "You are the most beautiful woman I have ever met," to which she gibed, "You don't get out much do you?" She was used to compliments, not from my father, mind you, but from everyone else. She had no reason to worry about losing her youthful appeal. She had always been beautiful, and no matter how many times she became a grandmother, that would never change. Any doubts she had about her youth slipping away from her were soon outweighed by the sheer joy her grandson Michael brought into her life.

It was soon after Michael was born that Ena came into my life. I had come to the conclusion that I needed some help with this baby. I had never even held one before Michael was born, and I was so ignorant about infants. Mom had not held a baby since I was born, and although she was relishing every moment with her grandchild, she was as ignorant as I was. Ena was a godsend. She did not live with us, which was uncommon in Jamaica, She arrived at work at nine in the morning but left at five in the afternoon, and during those hours she made my life a joy. She taught me how to bathe a baby, how to nurse, how to change a diaper, and everything I needed to reassure myself my child would survive in spite of me. She also did most of the housecleaning, washing, and ironing, and she became an invaluable member of our family. Ena was a second mother, a babysitter, a housekeeper, and a friend all rolled into one. Ena remained a close friend of my mother's and an integral part of our family until she retired and moved to New York in 2004.

CHAPTER 16

Bob Marley

In the early '70s, Jamaica had been totally independent from "imperialist" England for a decade, and even though crime was escalating, at this point, my parents still felt comfortable calling Jamaica home. Tony and I had bought a small, three-bedroom house in a fairly nice neighborhood called Alysham, and we welcomed our second son, Sean, into our lives with great joy. Again, I was so grateful to have Ena's help, and she quickly became a second mother to our newest baby, as she had done with Michael. Mom was thrilled to have a second grandson, and she arrived at my house almost every day to hold and feed the new baby.

The new house we had purchased for our expanding family cost all of $17,500. My generous father had given us the down payment, and somehow we were able to make the monthly mortgage even though Tony was earning only $3,500 per year. He had joined his father's prestigious law firm, Judah and Desnoes, and was basically working for him. I remember Tony going to his father one day and telling him he could not live on $3,500 with a newborn son, and Mike just said, "I started at the bottom rung of the ladder and so will you."

My husband countered, "Well, then I will have to look for work somewhere else," and he did. He was offered a great job to be the in-house lawyer for one of the most profitable and successful companies in Jamaica. His salary was to be the princely sum of $4,600 per annum. That was a huge 33 percent raise in pay, and Tony was just about to accept it when the senior partner of Mike's firm, Mr. Judah, announced that it was ridiculous for Tony to leave. Tony's father's hard-nosed decision was immediately overruled; Tony got his raise and remained a young associate at the firm of Judah and Desnoes.

I believe this was a good decision all around, especially because Tony would have never been able to make the claim that he was one of Bob Marley's lawyers. That's right, he was one of the lawyers that helped Bob Marley and his manager get off the ground and start receiving their rightful share in the royalties of his historically inspiring songs. Not very many people know this, but Bob Marley's father was a wealthy white Englishman, his mother a not-so-wealthy black Jamaican. Living with his mother with no support from his father, Bob grew up in poverty with a lot of angst. I believe that is why his songs are so moving. There are two interesting Bob Marley stories that my mother and I always loved to tell.

One day Bob came into the law office to do some estate paperwork with Tony and Mike. Mike asked Bob the simple question, "Are you married?" There was a long pause. Bob, as usual, was in a ganja fog, but that was not the reason for the hesitation; he was genuinely trying to figure out if he was married or not. Mike, always a bit impatient, was getting irritated by the long pause and again asked "Are you married?"

After more pensive silence, Bob finally announced, "Kinda."

At his point, Tony's father gruffly announced, "What do you mean, kinda? It is a simple question, either you're married or you're not"

Bob replied slowly, "Well, I kinda married to Rita."

Bob Marley had many children by many different women and was obviously not living a faithful married life to Rita, so I can understand why he was genuinely trying to figure out if he was legally married or not. Apparently he was, but you would never know it by his lifestyle.

Another great Bob Marley story was the day he came into the office and proudly presented my husband Tony with an autographed life-sized poster of himself. It read, "To Tony, from Bob Marley."

When we told our children that story years later, they got excited and announced, "Do you realize how much money you can get on eBay for that?"

Then they heard the rest of the story: in one of our moves from one house to another, the poster was put in the "excess clutter" category and thrown out. One decision meant a treasure was lost forever. Oh well, a potential fortune down the drain.

CHAPTER 17

"I come to kill yu, but I don't kill Catolics"

From 1962 until 1973, my life was good in Jamaica; almost everyone could sense some sort of economic progress. The governing Jamaica Labor Party (JLP) tried it's best to do a good job in stimulating the economy of the country as evidenced by a recorded 6 percent growth per annum.

The serious problem for Jamaica was that for the 90 percent of the population who were black and poor, the changes were not happening fast enough. With liberation from the British, the assumption was that instant wealth for all was imminent. Immediate economic uplift had been promised by campaigning politicians, so when it turned out not to be the case, frustration and anger among the underprivileged started to fester. You cannot pull yourself out of poverty by waving a magic wand of instant entitlement. It takes education, hard work, and discipline—three things that were sorely lacking among many of the youth of Jamaica who were still stuck in the ghetto. But their frustration was palpable, and the resentment and envy they acquired against anyone who was economically better off were slowly building. It really did not matter what color you were. If you drove a car or lived in a nice house you were considered rich and automatically became a target of envy.

One day, my longtime friend Rosanna, was driving through Kingston when she stopped at a red light. A barefoot man who had been standing at the side of the road for quite some time decided he was going to leisurely stroll across the road at the precise moment the light turned green. Rosanna was in a bit of a hurry, so she decided to blow her horn at him. That was a mistake; he stood in the middle of the road and started yelling obscenities and waving his machete at her in a threatening manner. But it's what he said that she found shocking. He shouted to her that the car she was driving today was going to be his tomorrow,

"Ah so it go, Michael Manley sey so!" It was of no importance to him that she had worked hard and saved up for years to be able to buy a little car for herself. That did not seem to matter. This man truly believed that it was now his right to take her car away and make it his—an act that in a civilized, law-abiding country would be called theft. This was now considered legal, and in his mind, he even had the approval of our political leaders to do so. *What was happening?*

What was happening was it was now 1974, and the new governing body in power was the People's National Party, led by Michael Manley, in many people's opinion, the one man who was about to ruin life for everyone in Jamaica: rich, poor, black, white, Chinese, or Indian, professionals and laborers alike.

Michael Manley, the son of Norman Manley, a wealthy black Jamaican, and Edna, a white Englishwoman, had studied at the London School of Economics where he embraced Marxist philosophy with enthusiasm. With great gusto, he came home to Jamaica and was elected prime minister in 1972. Once elected, he declared himself to be a democratic socialist. Most educated people just called it plain communism. With overpowering good looks and charisma, he convinced the entire population that if they voted for him, he would "empower the oppressed" by creating a "new heaven and a new earth" in Jamaica. But unlike Prime Minister Bustamante's plans for empowering the oppressed by creating economic growth, Michael Manley's idea was to redistribute the wealth by tearing down the capitalist system and creating a socialist regime. The oppressed would be liberated at last. This sounded very appealing; no one wanted to be oppressed. However, instead of redistributing the wealth by turning the "oppressed" into productive responsible citizens, he began to play the blame game and planted the seeds for racial and social tensions to grow. He declared the poverty and hardships that people were experiencing to be caused by wealthy capitalists—products of the ex-ruling British and the wicked imperialist Americans. In his speeches, he talked a lot about the "haves and have-nots" and pointed out with great eloquence that, for the most part, the have-nots were the oppressed, impoverished, black Jamaicans, and the haves were the lighter-skinned wealthier Jamaicans. Even if this was not his intent, instead of encouraging education and hard work for oppressed the way "Busta" had, he created fierce resentment toward economically successful Jamaicans of all color and especially toward anyone who was white.

Sure, there was inequality that needed to be fixed, but Manly took advantage of the young country's colonial history to further his socialist/communist cause, which in many opinions, eventually took the country down a path of total economic disaster. If he had hung on to a free-market philosophy, he could have tapped into the many resources Jamaica had, encouraged foreign investment and exports, grown the economy, and empowered the working class by creating new jobs. Jamaicans would benefit—black, white, rich, and poor—with endless possibilities for all to advance. But this was not to be. Manley called himself a socialist, but he and his left-wing thugs were determined to take Jamaica down a Cuban-style communist path. Instead of uniting all Jamaicans, he drove a wedge between the classes, feeding resentment and spawning hostile social riots and unrest.

I will never forget the first time Mom and I became victims of the racial hatred that I believe Michael Manley perpetuated. It took place in 1975. We were walking through a shopping-mall parking lot, minding our own business, and a man walked up to us and spat at our feet.

He shouted, "Go home, white woman, we nuh want yu here."

Mom and I were both quite taken aback. She just stood there, not knowing how to handle the situation. I, on the other hand, was ready to put up a fight and justify my presence.

I turned to him and said, "I am home; this is my home. I was born here, just like you."

He spat at us again and walked away in disgust. This was the first time in my life I felt truly unwelcome in the country I called home. I know I was white and he was black, but we were both Jamaicans. Wasn't there room for both of us? Why did he hate us so much? He didn't even know us.

But this was just the beginning. Racial and social prejudices began to soar throughout the island, and anyone could become a victim. Lighter-skinned Jamaicans were especially singled out for violent attacks. The violence was no longer confined to political gangs in the ghettos. It started spreading rapidly to all corners of the island. No neighborhood or area was immune from a random home invasion, and they were terrifying. At this point, no one in the family had yet become a victim of a violent crime, but many of our friends were not so fortunate.

Mom was visibly shaken one day when one of her good Irish friends arrived at the house to tell her she was leaving the island. She had been a victim of a horrific home invasion and said she couldn't sleep at night anymore and had become a nervous wreck. She felt the only solution was to leave. She had been alone at home in the kitchen when she was suddenly confronted by a large "rasta" man staring her straight in the face. It was during the day, so he must have slipped in through a door or window that had been carelessly left open. He was half stoned and very angry, and worst of all, he was wielding a large machete. She said she just stood there, petrified, as the intruder proceeded to yell at her. "Ah goin' to rape you, white woman, den ah goin' to kill yu," which is often what happened.

Surprisingly, my mother's friend said she somehow kept her wits about her and told him if he was going to kill her, she needed to say her Act of Contrition. This is a prayer Catholics say when they are about to meet their death. Immediately, she fell to her knees, made the sign of the cross and began to pray.

The man looked at her and said, "You is a Catolic?"

She said yes, she was, and continued to pray.

He turned around and walked out of the house, announcing, "I don't kill Catolics," leaving her unharmed.

As the friend related the story to my mother, she said a strange calm had come over her when the man told her of her fate, and she just went numb but felt she should start to pray. Miraculously, her prayers were answered that day, but I am sure it took a long time for her to recover from that traumatic experience. My mother was deeply disturbed at what had happened to her friend, not only because she was losing a close friendship, but also because of the stark realization that anyone could become a victim of senseless brutality, and if you were white, your chances were much higher. Mom's friend's life was spared that day, but she was one of the lucky ones.

A Canadian visitor who was staying with our neighbors up the road in Red Hills was not so lucky. A man broke into her bedroom in the middle of the night and violently raped her. It was such an upsetting experience, she left the country the very next day, and we never spoke of the brutal attack again.

Another close friend was robbed and murdered as he was walking along the palisades beach that led out to the airport. Just held up and shot at close range. All the gunmen got were a few dollars from the victim's wallet. Life had no value to these lawless criminals. Mayhem surged all around us, and the circle of crime was closing in quickly.

It is likely that Michael Manley, deep down, had good intentions for Jamaica when he became prime minister in the early 1970s. He did set some positive initiatives into motion, like attempting to stamp out illiteracy and providing free education for all. But I believe his downfall, and subsequently, the downfall for Jamaica, was trying to impose his socialist regime on a country that really needed a capitalist regime. Jamaica needed foreign investment and strong private manufacturing and agricultural industries to survive. Much to the US disapproval, he started to develop close friendships with the communists. His new best friend was Fidel Castro, and he often expounded, "I have walked to the mountaintop with Fidel." Taking a page from Castro's doctrine, Manley also banned ownership of all foreign assets. If you owned any foreign land or had a foreign bank account, especially in US dollars, you had to sell everything, bring the money back to Jamaica immediately, and convert all currency into Jamaican dollars.

What? I did not like the sound of that. Talk about putting a grinding halt to free enterprise and taking away personal liberties. This put everybody in a panic. It was beginning to look more and more like

Cuba. But for now, Jamaica still had a two-party political system. Surely the opposition would never allow Jamaica to fall into Castro's hands.

Not only had Manley broken the cardinal rule of pissing off the United States by chumming up to Castro and other socialist African leaders like President Julius Nyerere of Tanzania and that lunatic Gadaffy, he made the big mistake of thinking that if he sided with the communists, they would fund his social revolution. He turned down IMF loans from the West and relied solely on his communist friends to support his new welfare programs just as they had in Cuba. The problem was that the Soviet Republic had long run out of money for Cuba, much less Jamaica. Cuba certainly had no money for Jamaica, however, Castro did manage to send over lots of "doctors and teachers" to help build the country. These so called doctors and teachers tuned out to be nothing more than armed guerillas, Cuban thugs who, once they were on Jamaican soil, started building training camps in the mountains to teach the Jamaican thugs how to plan a successful revolution. They also started brainwashing the youth with their communist agenda of totalitarian control. The newly formed PNP Youth Organization was soaking it all up. They would become proficient in the art getting rid of political rivals or anybody who got in their way—as if the Jamaican political thugs needed any help to carry out their war of terror.

Manley's huge attempts to move Jamaica from a fairly stable capitalist society to a disastrously unstable socialist society, along with the promises of wealth that the politicians could not keep, turned the country so upside down that life would never be the same. All Jamaicans suffered the aftereffects of the growing social and racial violence, and eventually, many were forced, like us, to escape their precious island home.

I will always remember my father-in-law's comment, "I hate that man Manley. He tore my family apart and took my children away from me"

Even though disturbing things were happening in the land of my birth, we somehow kept pushing forward, armed with the lingering hope that surely, if the opposition political party failed to stop the communist march, the United States would never allow another Cuba so close to its shores.

The more pressing problem was the widespread violence that was encroaching rapidly. Although the awareness of the violence seldom left any of us, we somehow learned to manage the fear that followed us everywhere. Life had to go on, and it did.

Author and her Family 1969

CHAPTER 18

Succumbing to the island's hypnotic spell of adulterous affairs

After I was married, Mom and I remained very close. I was no longer living at home, but she drove down from Red Hills to meet me at least three times a week to catch up on things. We always did our shopping together, and she volunteered to babysit her young grandsons regularly. I thought I had kept pretty close tabs on her. That is why, when she told me, years later, that she had been having an affair with a married man during that time, I went into complete shock.

I was not angry that I was kept in the dark—after all, affairs are usually kept in the dark. It was really none of my business, and she had no obligation to talk to me about it, then or ever. We were adults now.

But I must say, I found the whole situation quite unbelievable. *My mother having an affair.* How intriguing. It had taken her twenty-odd years, but she had finally succumbed to the island's hypnotic spell of illicit adulterous affairs. She was indulging in the very behavior that had caused her to write to her parents years before, "This island is going to hell." Maybe she had already experienced hell on that island and so thought it justifiable to experience some heaven. It was all quite difficult for me to assimilate, and I remained in a state of disbelief for quite a while. If this was true, did it mean the long, obsessive, love affair with my father was finally over?

The tables sure had turned. My immediate thoughts were "vindication at last." But I was deeply curious as to whether my father ever knew about it, and if he did, what was his reaction? I soon found out that the married man she was having an affair with had been separated from his wife years before Mom had ever met him, so thank goodness the affair had not broken up their marriage. Once I knew that,

I was surprisingly happy for her. I don't think I could have condoned her behavior if she had broken up a marriage and caused another wife deep pain. I know she would never have done that. Once you have experienced that kind of pain, you never want to wish it on anybody else, and she knew heartache first hand. But I was thrilled at the thought that she had found someone to give her the attention and love that was so sorely lacking in her own marriage. Hopefully, she got to experience some well-deserved happiness, even if only for a few years. (I believe that is how long the affair lasted, but she would not divulge any more details to me except to tell me it had indeed taken place.) The mystery man apparently lived high up in the Blue Mountains with acres of coffee plantations all around his estate. The couple used to rendezvous at his mountaintop house where, I am told, the views of the city of Kingston and surrounding hillside were spectacular.

However, that is only half the story of my mother's intriguing affair. It gets even more complicated. I could tell it was very difficult for her to talk about it, especially to her children. I am sure she would have preferred to take her secret to the grave. So why *did* she reveal the truth about the illicit relationship with this mysterious married man with whom she had fallen in love? Well, as fate would have it, years later, my beautiful sister Bridget, decided to marry the son of Mom's lover. It was at that point, I believe, that my mother thought it prudent to tell her children what had taken place years before. It would be better coming from her personally than from a second-hand source, namely the new in-laws. The in-laws also found it prudent to tell their children at this time also, assumingly for the same reason. So now the truth was known by all the offspring, and two of these offspring were now going to marry each other. *Oh boy, what a mess.* Fortunately, this new revelation did not slow down plans for the wedding in the slightest. It just added some unexpected awkwardness. I was happy for Bridget; she was madly in love. I only hoped that when I met the new in-laws for the first time, they would remember that children are not responsible for their parents' behavior.

But to me, even by Jamaican standards, this was a pretty mixed-up situation. I found the whole thing quite incestuous frankly. Thank goodness Mom never got pregnant from this relationship. Just the thought that I could have had two half siblings, one on my father's side and one on my mother's side, ending up wanting to marry each other—*oh my God!* That would have been way too much to handle.

There is a famous Trinidadian calypso that was popular in the '70s entitled "Shame and Scandal in the Family." It is a story about a boy who wants to marry his true love and goes to his father for permission only to have his father tell him he can't marry her because "that girl is yu sista, but yu muddah don't know." Then the boy goes to his "muddah" and woefully tells her the sad truth. His "muddah" laughs and tells him he can go ahead and marry her because 'Yu daddy ain't yu daddy, but yu daddy don't know." The boy laments, "Woe is me. Shame and scandal in di fam-i-ly." A very amusing song that for some reason kept popping into my head as Mom was telling me her story. All of a sudden, the calypso's lyrics weren't so amusing—in fact, they started to sound way too familiar.

When the invitations to Bridget's wedding arrived, Mom graciously declined to attend, a wise decision. But my brother Peter and I wanted to be there and show Bridget support on her special day. I would be meeting her mother, Molly, for the first time, my father's lover from twenty-four years ago. I got even more stressed at the thought of meeting Bridget's father-in-law, Bobby, the man my mother had an affair with thirteen years earlier. It was enough to make my head spin.

The wedding was fantastic though. Dad may not have been there physically or emotionally very much for Bridget when she was growing up, but just like with my brother and I, he tried hard to make up for it in later years.

My problem was just trying to relax. Through the crowds, I kept getting glimpses of these two attractive people who had significantly affected my parents' lives so long ago. My curiosity was intense, and I was dying to meet them face to face. We were finally introduced, to my great relief, and the anxiety that had been building up quickly vanished.

Surprisingly, there was no embarrassment, no tension—it was as if I were meeting long-lost friends. They both seemed quite unperturbed about the whole situation. I think the only reason I was feeling so uneasy was because it was all so fresh in my mind. They had long since moved on, or at least that's the impression they gave me. I began to realize that my sister's new in-laws were pretty fun-loving people, my kind of people, and I knew we would all get along great. I started to relax—the rum punches really helped—and to accept the reality of our strangely intertwined families. Eventually, the tension completely eased, and I ended up having a really enjoyable time—inevitable at a good Jamaican wedding—even though the damn "shame and scandal in di fam-i-ly" lyric never stopped swirling around in my head.

My sister and brother-in-law have been happily married now for over twenty-eight years now, and my husband and I often spend Christmas with them. Bridget is an amazing cook, and she puts on a lavish Christmas dinner; it is the one time a year when all of her in-laws get together. I have gotten quite used to our uniquely connected families, but I have to admit, it did take some adjustment. Many times in the past I would sit across the Christmas table looking at Molly, Bridget's mother, the one my father had an affair with, and then I would make eye contact with Bridget's mother-in-law, Nora, the estranged wife of the man my mother had an affair with. I would squirm a little bit and wonder: were they feeling as awkward as I was? My parents have both passed away now, and so has Bobby, Bridget's father-in-law. Today, at the Christmas table, we are much more comfortable with each other, but whenever I am with them, even after all these years, the haunting calypso's lyrics keep popping into my head.

I never found out if Dad knew about my mother's affair at the time it was happening, although I assumed he did, but I wanted to know for sure. So one day, I plucked up the courage to ask Nora, the separated wife of Mom's lover and now Bridget's mother-in-law. I knew she would not mind talking about it, because her relationship with her husband had long since been over when this all took place (although, like my parents, they had never divorced). She told me that indeed Dad did know about it from the very beginning, and he was absolutely livid.

One night, while the affair was still going on, Nora bumped into Dad at a party, and neither of them was with his or her respective spouse. Dad verbally attacked Nora, barking at her, "Do you know your husband has stolen my wife away from me? What are you going to do about it, Nora?" He was wild with jealously. I can just imagine what people around thought as they overheard the confrontation. *Was that Tom O'Brien accusing someone of stealing his wife? Talk about the pot calling the kettle black.*

Nora said she told him that she was happy for them and so should he be. "Get over it Tom" she told him.

I know for a fact that my jealous father would never have "gotten over it" and could never have been happy for them. Everyone knew he had no right to make demands from Mom after what he had put her through, but apparently he tried.

As I look back, other happenings around the time of the affair started to make sense to me. It was around then that Mom told me she was thinking of divorcing my father. She had saved a little money and decided she would go to England for a while. I was shocked but also proud of her. Finally, she was standing up to Dad and taking charge of her own life. I had always assumed her decision was based on my father taking up with yet another young Jamaican "lassie" (as Mom used to call his girlfriends), and my mother had just had enough. *More power to her,* I had thought. *She should have made the break a long time ago.* Little did I know, there was a lot more brewing than I could have ever imagined. I am guessing now that Mom's affair had ended and life at home had become intolerable. She needed to get away, and she did just that.

No longer was she the meek, innocent, young wife that my father had summoned across the Atlantic so many years ago to that godforsaken place. Maeve Daly O'Brien had endured a lot—betrayal, heartache, a life threatening illness and many third-world-country challenges—forcing her to grow up and toughen up. When she left the shores of Ireland twenty-odd years earlier, she could never have imagined or recognized the person she was to become. Although she never gained financial independence from Dad in all those years, Mom developed a social independence that enabled her to make her own decisions, no longer needing his approval for every move.

With this support system, she summoned the fortitude to make the break, and she set off for London to live with one of the many good friends in her social network, June. June was the friend who Maeve had helped escape her unhappy marriage years before by smuggling her out of Jamaica unbeknownst to her cheating husband. After she had left Jamaica, June had subsequently married a very caring Englishman, and they both welcomed my mother into their warm home with open arms. June had never forgotten what my mother had done for her, and they had remained loyal friends ever since. Now June was repaying the favor.

Finally, my mother was championing her own cause, although I am sure Dad did not approve and would never have backed her plan. He would have made it as difficult as possible for her. Not only was this a blow to his male ego, it was embarrassing for him too. Dad had always kept up the façade of a quasi-healthy marriage, certainly to his mother and family back in Ireland and to anyone in Jamaica whom he could fool. But when one's wife just picks up and leaves, something is definitely wrong. One can't keep up appearances when that happens.

On our O'Brien family tree, in seven generations and hundreds of marriages, there was not a single divorce, and Dad did not want to be the first. But Mom didn't really care what he wanted at this stage. She was determined to make the break. She headed off to her good friend in London with very few resources to fall back on, but at least she was off.

I am sure this stint in London was my mother's way of proving to Dad (and more so to herself) that she could survive without him, but what courage this must have taken. Mom had never held a job and had no professional training of any kind. She knew she had limited energy, but she was still determined to try to make a go of it. She ended up waitressing in a local coffee shop near June's house, which proved to be very hard work for her. Mom was not used to manual labor, especially where she had to serve people and do it quickly. She was on her feet all day, pouring coffee to rushing customers in a fast-paced bustling city.

She certainly would not have minded the subservient role, my mother was never a snob, however I know the routine must have been very challenging for her. She never really made a lot of money in London, especially as she could only manage about five hours of work a day, but at least she finally had her own income, small as it was, and she seemed to manage. Even though she was staying with a friend and had no housing expenses to speak of, this little income did give her a huge feeling of financial freedom.

Maeve in England—1974

CHAPTER 19

Why is Castro visiting the island?

M om had chosen a good time to make her break from her unhappy marriage, because while she was off in England trying to figure out if she could survive as a single woman, life in Jamaica was becoming more and more intolerable.

As if the excessive crime was not nerve-racking enough, sometime in the mid-70s, a rumor reverberated around the island that seven prominent Jamaican families had been targeted to be murdered. A number of lawyers were supposedly on the hit list too. No one was quite sure who the seven families were or which lawyers had been chosen to be slain, but this rumor had everyone on high alert. I am sure these threats of terror were coming from the far-left corner of the PNP, where Manley's communist cohorts were diligently plotting their way to power.

It was a safe assumption that my family was not one of the targeted seven, as the O'Briens were far from prominent, but my husband Tony was a lawyer, and I *did* know some prominent people. I got a sick feeling in the pit of my stomach when I heard about these new threats and started experiencing overwhelming panic attacks. Which one of my friends was going to be murdered, and was my husband next? Even if I personally knew no one on the list, the situation was very frightening. Not only was there a constant fear of becoming a victim of a random murder by lawless thugs, now you could become a victim of a violent crime, deliberately plotted by corrupt, power-hungry fanatics. If these "politicians" thought you might stand in the way of their communist plans for Jamaica, they could just bump you off. The scary thing was that you could be put on the list for simply speaking out in opposition to their plans to take the country down the democratic socialist path, which made you a threat. These men were ruthless and dangerous, and in their pursuit of power, they had lost their sense of right and wrong.

One day, my husband Tony came home from work in the middle of the afternoon.

"What are you doing home so early?" I asked him.

He nonchalantly said there had been a bomb scare in his building, and everyone had been ordered to evacuate. *Oh my God, maybe they really after were him.*

"Did everyone get out?" I asked.

Well, everyone except his father Mike, who was still sitting at his desk working. Mike had declared the whole thing to be "total nonsense" and refused to leave. How typical that was of my father-in-law. I am not sure whether he really had no fear or was just in total denial of the ominous changes taking over his beloved country. As time went on, the latter proved to be true. I have always thought Mike should have paid more attention to those initial warning signs. He should have prepared himself and his family for the inevitable. If so, maybe he could have avoided the terrifying ordeal that was to come a few years later.

At this stage of Jamaica's history, so much violence and terror permeated the country that everyone felt the need to own a gun. The criminals wanted guns to carry out their acts of violence, and ordinary citizens wanted guns to defend themselves against those criminals. Mind you, neither Dad nor Tony believed in owning one. Too many times burglars would break into a house to steal the guns, and the owner would end up being shot by his own weapon. So we never owned one (and never will). In the mid-70s, there were so many guns floating around Jamaica and so many gun-related crimes that the government in its "deliberate wisdom" declared a State of Emergency and formed the famous Gun Court, banning the possession of all guns. There was an amnesty period to turn in firearms, and if, after that period, you were caught with even a single bullet on you, there was no trial; you went straight to jail.

Michael Manley's party actually locked up over five hundred people without a trial, most of them JLP supporters, right before the elections of 1976, so that explains a lot of the reasoning behind their "State of Emergency." It was one way of getting rid of the two-party political system and the opposing political party. Did they really think "Gun Court" would somehow change the heart of the violent criminal and make him magically turn in his weapons and stop the rampage of brutality? *Give me a break.*

It was during this pivotal year that the Manley government took away yet another personal freedom that upset many people and changed lives forever. At this time, Jamaican citizens were free to travel, however Manley imposed a new law limiting one's personal travel allowance to a mere fifty US dollars a year. That could barely buy a meal. This single act caused so much consternation that I believe it was the final straw that compelled a lot of hard-working, law-abiding citizens to leave the country. Everyone was in a state of perplexity and anxiety. Questions were on everyone's mind: Why couldn't they spend their hard-earned money wherever they wanted to spend it? If this was the direction the country was going, how valuable would the Jamaican dollar be in the future? Could it devalue rapidly, like what had happened in Mexico with many losing their life savings and net worth? Were more personal freedoms going to be taken away, one by one, to slowly make citizens prisoners in their own country? Why was Fidel Castro visiting the island, and why were the government ministers visiting Moscow?

This was a serious situation. Not only had Manley ordered everyone to keep 100 percent of their currency in Jamaican dollars, but now you couldn't exchange them for any other currency if you wanted to travel outside of Jamaica. This new ban on foreign exchange caused such a state of panic on the island that people were racking their brains to come up with creative ways to smuggle US dollars out of the country. We had seen what the Cubans had gone through and did not want to end up in an inner tube washed up onto the Florida shores penniless with only the clothes on our backs. With these new laws, citizens were pushed into criminal activities just to preserve their own hard-earned money. They were turning up at the airport in fake casts stuffed with US dollars that had been bought on the black market. Suitcases had extra linings sewn in. Couches and chairs were being shipped abroad with dollars crammed into the cushions. Soon the officials caught on to the smuggling and began random strip searches of travelers at the airport. If you were caught with one US dollar on you, you could go to jail. It was scary.

Of course, my Honest Abe husband and his father both decided they could never break the law. They were "Officers of the Court" and could lose their professional licenses if they got caught. Honest to a fault and unlike many others around them, they never took a single US dollar out of the country. This shortsighted decision proved to be the wrong one and resulted in great financial hardships later on in life, especially for my stepmother-in-law Christine.

So, between Michael Manley's Marxist/socialist regime that was spending millions of dollars it did not have, the panic among the hard-working, educated middle and upper classes who started to drain the country of whatever money they could get their hands on in anticipation of a quick escape, and the out-of-control brutal violence, Jamaica was an economic train wreck waiting to happen.

History shows, you cannot have a social revolution and create wealth for the poor without a growing economy, and you cannot have a growing economy if you don't have the capital investors to ignite competition and creativity. Do whatever you can to keep the flow of money coming into the island; do not run it out with threats of nationalization and heavy taxes and widespread corruption. Michael Manley forgot that in order to "redistribute the wealth" you had to have wealth in the first place. And the little bit of wealth Jamaica did have was rapidly flying off the island.

I believe that Michael Manley is the man most responsible for Jamaica's economic collapse and the subsequent self-destruction that my island home suffered; I know many people share the same sentiment. He may not have thought of himself as a communist, after all he always claimed to be a democratic socialist, but he allowed himself to be surrounded by totalitarian psychopaths, ruthless men who were determined to turn Jamaica communist with or without him.

My father-in-law Mike, like many older Jamaicans, hated Manley and cursed him every day for splitting up their families. But I am neither a politician nor a historian. I am sure there are political and historical scholars who are much more informed than I am and might disagree with my conclusions. However, what I know for sure is that during those years, an atmosphere of instability and fear was living in every cell of my body. I also know it was rapidly creeping into the lives of all law-abiding, hard-working Jamaicans, black and white, rich and poor alike. The future became uncertain, the poor were getting poorer, the shortages were getting worse, the country was going bankrupt, and crime was off the charts. But the one thing I promised myself, assuming we survived the situation, was that I would never raise my children in a communist country. The experiences of Cuba were way too close for comfort.

CHAPTER 20

If you bite the hand that feeds you, you go hungry

In 1975, my mother returned home to Jamaica from England. She had been gone almost a year, and I got a phone call from Dad to tell me the news. He actually sounded excited, so I made the assumption that a truce had been formed and all was well again—at least for a while. Maybe the only thing that happened was winter was dragging on, and Mom forgot how miserable British winters could be, but whatever the reason, she was back. Quite honestly, I was getting a bit sick of the constant back and forth between those two. And at this point in my life, I was focusing most of my attention on my own marriage and family. I dutifully welcomed her home, but I never really got into any details with her about why she returned. I know Mom could have survived financially if she'd wanted to, especially after my grandmother Mammy Daly died and left her the valuable old family house in Dublin. Even Mom's conservative Catholic mother must have realized there was a good chance her daughter might break away from her marriage and need money. Mom had indeed broken away, but yet she chose not to remain free. At least this time it was she who was coming back to Dad. She had the control, so I guess she'd made her point.

When she returned, I could see a difference in my father's attitude toward her. Surprisingly, he was not angry at all; in fact he seemed very relieved and a bit humbled—at least temporarily. He knew that if he wanted to stay married, which he did, he had better not take her for granted any more. The balance of power was slowly leveling out.

I was glad to have Mom home, but I believe she was quite shocked at changes she found when she returned to Jamaica. To me, they had been gradual, so not so disturbing, but she had been away for one year, living in a country where, for the most part, life functioned normally. I think she realized the changes in attitudes toward white Jamaicans when one morning we went clothes shopping. As we browsed around the store, we noticed the sales clerks milling around nearby but being very aloof and totally ignoring us. The more my mother tried to get assistance, the more she was ignored. I guess I had gotten used to this treatment, because I did not expect any assistance. I just picked out what I wanted and went to the checkout counter, knowing I would have a long wait but they would eventually take my money. Mom had gotten used to store clerks who actually bent over backward to help their customers, so she was quite taken aback by this new "ignore the customer" form of salesmanship.

After the frustrating attempt at shopping, we went for our mandatory cup of tea at the Sheraton Hotel, where we used to go quite regularly in the past. Mom always felt that "nice cup of tea" would change her whole outlook on life, which it frequently did. Not quite as effective as a whiskey, straight up with a dash of water, but during daylight hours, tea was her medicine of choice; it did the job most of time. We sat down at the table and waited and waited, but no one came over to take our order. It was as if we were invisible. We could see the waitresses huddled together having a great chat in the corner, totally ignoring us. Then a black couple came into the restaurant, sat down, and immediately got served. Mom and I just looked at each other and knew: this was more than just slow service; this was deliberate. The waitresses were sending a signal that said we were not welcome there, and they were going to let us know it in no uncertain terms. Eventually, we did begrudgingly get served but not without a long wait. If it had not been for the fact that my mother was panting for her precious cup of tea, we would have walked out. Although the feeling we got from the waitress was more of contempt, not superiority, this reverse prejudice that we experienced was extremely unpleasant. I can never truly feel the indignities African Americans suffered fighting for their civil rights in the '50s and '60s when they were refused service in diners in the South, but, in a very small way, I can appreciate how they must have felt.

What was fueling the fire of this animosity toward white people in Jamaica was that Michael Manley was preaching to all under his regime, "There will be no more masters and no more servants," once again, triggering the memory of slave days and stirring up old hatreds. However it had been 150 years since slavery had been abolished, and the relationship today was not between masters and servants but more between customers and employees. As long as there is a need, there will always be a service industry. There will always be people aiding other people, whether it be a housekeeper, waitress, store clerk, doctor, or lawyer, such is the makeup of our society; in my opinion, it has nothing to do with slavery.

However, the memories of slavery can be very painful and any reference can fuel angry resentments. These were tumultuous times in Jamaica, and the left-wing politicians were stirring it all up, focusing on past transgressions instead of future opportunities. The hostile attitude toward white customers was permeating the entire country. No industry felt the economic impact more severely than the tourist industry. Guests in hotels were being ignored and treated disrespectfully. There were numerous complaints about excruciatingly slow waits in the restaurants and harassments in the streets. As a result, the tourism slacked off in the late '70s and early '80s. Jamaicans did not realize, if you bite the hand that feeds you, you go hungry.

CHAPTER 21

How did they get through the burglar bars?

At this stage, Tony and I were still hoping, against all odds, that things would get better in Jamaica. He was now a partner in the law firm and pursuing a successful career. We had two great children who were attending an excellent Catholic grade school and doing quite well. I had gone back to work part-time and loved my computer programming. We had a wonderful group of friends whom we saw every day. For every aspect of our lives that we had control over, we felt we were doing all the right things and making the right decisions, and we were happy. However, looming over our lives was the part that we had absolutely no control over. We felt as if we were being swept along in a tidal wave of political unrest, and the more we resisted, the more powerless we got. There were vicious forces out there unraveling the constitution, the two-party system, and anything that even smelled of a capitalistic economy. The churning waters were spawning such racial hatred and tension that our entire future in Jamaica became questionable. But still we clung to the hope that somehow common sense would prevail, the two-party system would stand, and we would be saved from the government's misguided socialist policies.

My husband and I had sold our little house with the hope of purchasing a bigger home in a nice neighborhood called Manor Park. The Manor Park home was not completed, so in the interim, we moved back to my parents' home in Red Hills. Both my dad and mom were thrilled at the prospect of having their grandkids living with them, and they immediately volunteered to build an extra wing onto the house to accommodate us all. One thing about my Dad, even with all his flaws, he was the most generous, hospitable man I have ever known, and he welcomed us into his house with open arms. An entire second floor to my parents' home had already been added by my brother Peter when he was living there as a young adult, so when we went to live with my parents, they moved upstairs to the apartment Peter had built, while we moved in downstairs to the newly remodeled addition. It was while we were living there that we experienced two traumatic events that, as far as I was concerned, were to seal our fate forever.

One morning, both my husband and I woke up feeling groggy and somewhat dazed. As we started to focusing and moving about, we realized it was ten o'clock, the kids were in their beds asleep, the house was wide open, and all the electronics and numerous other items in the house were missing. We had been robbed!

But why did we not wake up, and how did they get in? After all, at this stage, burglar bars were installed on every window and door. When the police arrived, they examined everything and told us the only way burglars could have entered was through a very small window high above a regular window. It was the only window in the house that did not have a burglar bar across it. But it was only about seven inches wide, so we had never considered it a vulnerable point of entry. This tiny window was directly above the bed our four-year-old son Michael was sleeping on. When we pieced it all together, we concluded that a small kid must have crawled through the window and climbed right on top of Michael and his bed. The kid then opened the house for the rest of the gang. But why had we not heard anything, and why did our four-year-old son not wake up when someone stepped on his bed? The police informed us that we had been drugged. This was a new modus operandi that burglars were doing, where they filtered some sort of drug through the air conditioning vents to knock us out and make us sleep while they robbed the house. I really did not care that the robbers had taken our TV, our stereo, our record player, etc. I did not even care that Tony and I had been drugged; at least we were still alive. What really upset me was that our young children had also been victims to this drugging. What had been put in their little systems, and what potentially fatal things would have been done to them if they had woken up? I was no longer intimidated, and even though I was grateful our lives had been spared, I was furious.

Then, about a month after that, my mother and I were alone at home on a Sunday afternoon with my two sons, Michael and Sean, when I looked out the window and saw the entire back lawn on fire. I had no idea how the fire started, but it was spreading to larger bushes, and with the flames getting higher and higher, it was rapidly approaching the house. I went into a panic and started running around holding the hose in one hand and a phone in the other trying to squelch the fire and to reach Tony who was about twenty miles away sailing in Kingston Harbor. Mom ran to the hose pipe to turn the valve on. When you turn on a water pipe in Jamaica, you learn to hold your breath in anticipation, never knowing what's really going to happen, but in this instance, I was very relieved that water actually did come out at the other end of the hose. I knew I would not reach Tony in time—it was way before the days of cell phones—so Mom and I had to make all the decisions to try to save our house. The addition my father had built onto the concrete house was made entirely of wood, so I knew the house was vulnerable.

Although I had little faith that the fire department would get there quickly, I did call them. In the meantime, Mom and I did everything to keep the fire at bay: spraying it with the hose and incorporating the kids help to pour as many buckets of water on the fire as fast as they could manage. To my relief, the fire brigade did arrive and were able to put the fire out before it had reached the perimeter of the house.

It was while we were all standing around after the fire was out that a strange scenario took place. I was thanking the firemen for helping me save our house when one of them looked at Michael and Sean, my two young sons, and said to them, "What you white boys doin' here anyway? Yu know we no want yu here." Michael just looked up at his potential hero in confusion. I angrily told the fireman to talk to me if he had something to say, not to my children. He repeated what he had said.

I told him in patois, "A fimmi country too, I man bawn ya and dem boys bawn ya too," which means it is also *our country* because we were all born here.

Well, the firemen went off in disgust, and as they walked back to their fire truck, they spat on the ground and again repeated, "We nuh want yu here, yu nor yu white sons."

I was stunned by the whole scenario. The adrenalin was still flowing from the threat of the fire; to have the emergency responders be so hostile toward my children tripled that adrenalin in my system.

My sons' ancestors on Tony's side of the family had been in Jamaica since 1730. They were very much Jamaican, and it was their birthright to live there. My blood was boiling. Mom, too, was visibly shaken by the whole scene. These men were supposed to protect citizens, not alienate them. After all, they had trained to keep citizens safe. Sure, they put the fire out this time, but after the insults, I began to realize we could not rely on any part of the system to protect us anymore—we were on our own. We had become outcasts in our own country, unwelcome and unwanted.

What sealed our fate was what happened one afternoon as I was driving the children home from school. I was stopped at a red light when I felt something hard bounce off my car, and then I felt another blow. I looked over to see a man standing at the side of the road throwing stones at us. *What the hell?* He was cursing at us as he threw each stone, yelling at us to get out of his country. The children were scared,

"What's he doing, Mommy? Why is he throwing rocks at us?" I was so upset I could not answer them. I drove off with numerous dents in the car, knowing the dents that stranger put in my heart were much deeper. That incident was the last straw. Was this what life was going to be like from now on?

Tony and I could handle the insults, but when it started to involve our children, we both acknowledged it was time to think about leaving the country. We did not want Michael and Sean growing up with such hostility, and we knew it would only get worse. They were young, but they still picked up on the tension and fear that surrounded us. Although we would try to shelter them from the talk about the latest political blunder or the latest violent murder, it was impossible. Such topics were being repeated over and over on television, on the radio, and around every dinner table in Jamaica. Politics and crime were on everyone's lips, and the children were not stupid, they knew what was going on. Every night I would put the boys to bed early, and invariably at around eleven o'clock, Tony and I would hear the door of our bedroom open and two little figures would appear with bedclothes and pillow in tow. They would curl up on the floor as close to our bed as possible and settle down to sleep, thinking we had not noticed them. They often told me that they were too scared to sleep in their room by themselves. I guess they thought Mom and Dad would protect them. The problem was, Mom and Dad were not so sure they could protect them at all.

I called my mom, sat her down, and told her the time had come; we had to leave Jamaica. I could actually see the huge sigh of relief on her face. Although the future was totally unknown, we had to start making plans to depart our beloved home, and thank goodness, both my mother and father totally agreed.

CHAPTER 22

The illusive green card

The decision to leave Jamaica had been made, but questions were swirling around in my head. Where would we go? How would we earn a living? How could we start a new life with only fifty US dollars? We had no money outside of Jamaica, but we knew we had no choice.

Around this same time, my mother's "twin" sister, Auntie Gina, had decided it was finally time to divorce her philandering husband. She announced to all that she was leaving him and going to live in Miami where she had family. I am sure my mother felt devastated at the thought of losing her best friend, her only daughter, and her grandchildren to a faraway land all at the same time. Mind you, Miami is not that far away, but Mom was well aware of the deep loneliness that follows separation from friends or family. After all, she had lived it. Even though times had changed since the '50s, and air travel was much cheaper and more available, a huge sense of loss still came over her. She never spoke about it, but I believe it was at that very moment that she quietly started drawing up the plans for her own escape.

The thing was, around that time many other families our age were also planning their exodus from Jamaica. In fact, in 1975 alone, over thirty thousand Jamaicans left their country. So even though the thought of starting life in a new country was scary for us, at least we had the backing of our peers. It had to be done—we were all in this together—and somehow this gave us all some comfort. Mom had no such support system.

Tony's family was not as supportive as mine when they heard the news that we were thinking of leaving. Unlike my parents, they had never immigrated to another country, and to them, the unknown was way too risky. Tony's grandfather Iya (as his grandkids used to call him), who absolutely adored his grandson, went into a severe depression when he heard of our plans. He was a real worrywart, and he kept telling my husband he would end up sweeping streets if he moved to America or England. He said Tony would be a *nobody*, unable to earn a living. Iya also told us it would be a huge financial step backward. What would happen to his grandson's lucrative law career? The legal system was totally different in the United States; all his education would go to waste. Iya's heart was breaking, and he was devastated at the thought of losing such a big part of his family. He had been widowed a few years earlier, so I kept telling him he could come and live with us wherever we ended up, but he was now in his eighties, and he kept repeating, "You cannot uproot an old tree."

Tony's father Mike was also devastated, although we knew he had a hard time expressing it. Mike was very proud of Tony's partnership in the law firm, and the move would be a big loss, not only to the family but also to the firm. Even though it was inevitable that this would tear the family apart, deep down, the harsh reality was that it was the right thing to do—for the safety of our children and the security of our future. Both sets of parents knew this, and although it was painful, they accepted our decision. Iya was the only one who really could not handle it.

It was a sad situation, but many of our friends had come to the same conclusion that we had: for the sake of the children's future, we had to leave. Tony had already decided that if he stayed in Jamaica he could not sit on the sidelines and watch the political destruction of his country. He would have had to get involved. In fact, he had already written a number of letters to the national newspaper, *The Daily Gleaner*, decrying "the rising incidence of crime and the seeming general breakdown of social order" and "government's apparent indifference to do anything about it." All of his letters had been published and were drawing unwelcome attention to him, not to mention the family.

Tony knew that if he continued, he would probably lose his life. He was the wrong color, and he was not a communist and nowhere close to being a socialist. These new politicians were ruthless, and anyone who got in their way could be snuffed out with no remorse. After all, as a lawyer, Tony was supposedly already on a hit list. With a wife and two young children to think about, he could not take more risks. The only conclusion was that we had to get out while we could.

It is a strange feeling when you realize that you have made the decision to pick up and leave the land of your birth—leaving everything and everyone you have ever known—and move to a totally new country, hoping for a better life and praying you are doing the right thing. I developed a new appreciation for what my parents had gone through twenty-five years earlier when they decided to leave Ireland.

Huge decisions had to be made, all of which we knew would affect our family's life forever. Our friends would be forever changed. Our future would be forever changed. Within our wide circle of friends, many had come to the same conclusion to leave; we knew we would end up scattered all over the globe, and some of us would never see each other again. It was too painful to think about. We had to stay focused on the monumental hurdles facing us—planning our escape, choosing the right country, hoping that country would accept us, and then finding a way to survive there.

This was now the main topic of conversation at every social gathering we attended. After the obligatory dissecting of the latest political blunder and cursing the political leaders, all we could talk about was where were we going to go and which country was our future going to be in. Mom was paying close attention to our decision-making process, because she knew she would want to end up wherever we ended up.

Jamaica is an ex-British colony. It was easy to emigrate to Britain, and it was where Tony gotten his law degree, so choosing England should have been a no brainer for us. Yet it was also easy selecting Canada because it was a Commonwealth country like Jamaica. For a lot of our friends, Canada was their choice, and many ended up in Toronto or Vancouver. However, although my heritage tells me I am an Irish colleen, my spirit tells me, even today, I am 100 percent an island gal. After growing up in the warm Caribbean, no way was I was going to live in a rainy, cold, gray country. I knew I had to have sunshine. I had to have warmth.

Also, I knew I did not want to be shoveling snow and wearing raincoats for most of the year. My brother Peter had gone to the

University of Toronto, and I kept remembering the stories about his eyeballs freezing one winter when it was so cold. I knew I never wanted my eyeballs to freeze.

Australia and New Zealand were other Commonwealth countries that we talked about a lot, because Tony's law degree would be recognized there. But enticing as they were, they were far away from everything we had ever known. Some of our friends did end up in Australia, and to this day, we've never gotten to see them.

For me, the only country to live in was the United States of America, even though it was going to be the most difficult location to start over in. The educational system was so different from the British system, and Tony's law degree would not be honored there. Still, I just knew that if we could get in, it would be the best decision we would ever make.

Before the limitation of fifty dollars a year for one's travel allowance, I had often accompanied Tony and his sailing partner, William, on their excursions to America. We had seen Florida, Texas, the East Coast, California, and the Puget Sound off Seattle—pretty much anywhere there was water to sail, he had sailed it. Even though we were always on a shoestring budget, whenever he was competing, I was exploring. I went everywhere I could, and I was falling in love with the United States, a country that I still believe today is the greatest in the world. I loved everything about America, and I knew I wanted to raise my family there. Mom was delighted we had chosen America, because she also loved the country and felt it was the right decision.

The hard part was getting in. The illusive "green card" that was needed to live and work there was as precious as gold and very difficult to come by, especially for Jamaicans. But where there's a will, there's a way. I convinced Tony not to go anywhere in America where our eyeballs would freeze, so we agreed it had to be in the Sunbelt. We immediately started the long paperwork process to acquire our green cards. We did not know if we would get accepted, but we were going to try. Strangely, my parents made no attempt to apply for a green card themselves. I guess they knew they had their safety net of being able to return to Ireland, even though Dad had no intention of ever returning to Ireland or anywhere else for that matter. He was going to remain in his beloved Jamaica for as long as he could.

At the time, for immigration purposes, the United States had divided up the world into sections, and each year, they would issue an allotted number of green cards to citizens of each country in each section. It just so happened that Dad, in his infinite wisdom and unbeknownst to me, had registered me as an Irish citizen when I was born, so *voila!*, I had dual citizenship. At that time, there were far fewer people from Ireland applying for their green cards than there were from Jamaica, so for us to be able to fall under the Irish quota was a huge help.

It was a tedious process with huge mountains of paperwork and numerous medical exams, police background checks, questionnaires, and interviews—and then came the long wait. During the two years it took for the immigration papers to go through, the situation in Jamaica only got worse. Garrison communities of rival political gangs grew larger and more violent every day, and this violence was spreading like wildfire. The government was going broke and unable to help anyone, not even its most desperate citizens. Hundreds of young boys and girls with no hopes of employment were left to mill around in the streets all day long with nothing to do, a situation ripe for gang leaders to take advantage of. They started brainwashing these young people into joining their gangs and committing to a life of drugs and crime in return for financial security for their families. When you have nothing to lose, an idea like this can sound very appealing, so the garrison neighborhoods grew and so did the gangs.

Along with the gangs, the anti-white sentiment was growing too, and the constant threat of attack never left us. I still remember the muscles in my body being in a constant state of tension, which, surprisingly, the body can get quite used to.

There had been no more bomb threats in my husband's law offices, and he seemed to be flying under the political radar for a while, which was good. I, on the other hand, had more opportunity for encountering danger and was more exposed. I had always done work with orphans and young mothers, and I couldn't stop now when the need was even greater during these difficult times. My work often took me to parts of town I really should not have been in. But that was where the orphans were and where the desperately poor people lived. Still, I never took careless risks, never travelled by myself, and was always aware of my surroundings at all times. The sad thing is that most poor Jamaicans are very loving, friendly people who appreciate anything you do for them and welcome you with open arms. But you just never knew when you would run into a" bad boy" or gang member who wouldn't hesitate to shoot you or chop you up on the spot. Thankfully, I never encountered a bad boy or gang member. However, I did have one unnerving incident that was close.

I was approached one day by a crazy dreadlocks man wielding a machete and threatening to "chop up di white whoman."

It was a blisteringly hot day in Kingston, and I had been out in the sun for a while. The sweat was dripping down my face, and I was exhausted. When this man approached me, I had had just about enough stress for one day, and I just put my hands on my hips, pulled myself up tall and shouted back at him, "Yu wan to chop mi up, den come chop mi up, right now, right here, chop mi up *RIGHT NOW!*" He was so startled at my reaction, and probably my Jamaican accent, he ran off. It is true what they say: in a life-threatening situation you react with either fight or flight. I guess my fight instincts took over just as they had years earlier when the man grabbed me on the beach. I was lucky that it worked once again, but it was still scary. You never knew which time they were just bluffing and which time they would actually chop you up into pieces.

Another frustrating state of affairs we were forced to put up with during those two years was not in any way life-threatening, but still, to me and Mom, it was very annoying. Because of the ban on foreign exchange, imports into the island had stopped, and the shelves in the supermarkets were almost completely bare. I remember at one point going to my usual store to buy tampons, and to my shock, there were none to be had. Not one box of tampons could be found in any store in Kingston. This shortage was beyond frustrating. I think every woman can relate to this.

Then I heard a rumor that a hotel in Ocho Rios was selling tampons in its gift shop. I called one of my close girlfriends, and excitedly, we jumped into my car for a three-hour drive over the mountain to the North Coast in search of the illusive tampon.

Sure enough, one of the big chain hotels had brought in a case of tampons for its hotel guests and had them for sale. You would have thought they were gold. Posing as hotel guests, we bought every box on the shelf and then got in the car and drove three hours back to Kingston, very pleased with our windfall. It seems a bit crazy now. I really could have survived without tampons, but you would be surprised how desperate and frustrated you feel when you discover you can't have something you really want. It makes you want it all the more, and it becomes forbidden fruit.

The other big comfort I missed was cereal. Experiencing an inexplicable sense of loss when I could no longer purchase my favorite Raisin Bran or Corn Flakes, I began to crave them all the more. Everything else that we were now unable to buy in the stores did not bother me; it was just those two items, the illusive tampon and the vanishing cereal, that really upset me. Today my pantry is overflowing with cereal, more boxes that can be finished before the expiration date. It's as if I have a subconscious fear that Kellogg's is going to go out of business, and I will be left cereal-less once again, pining for my Frosted Flakes. Weird and silly, I know.

For Mom, of course, it was the cigarettes. I guess when imports stopped, everybody missed their own special luxuries, but I think nobody suffered more than the smokers. During this time, I was so glad I had given up smoking at four years old and never taken up the addictive habit as an adult. When cigarettes were added to the long list of banished goods, the smokers started to go crazy, and included in that group was, of course, Mom. I truly felt sorry for her; she was forced to take some pretty desperate measures, legally and illegally, to get her hands on a packet of Benson and Hedges. I remember her driving around town for hours in search of a street vendor on the side of the road who would sell single cigarettes. Even one cigarette at a time was better than none.

CHAPTER 23

Jamaica Farewell

The two years we were waiting for our green card went by excruciatingly slow, and then one day we got the magic letter from the US Embassy: "Please report to the embassy at 9:00 a.m. Tuesday morning for your final interview."

I can still recall the excitement we felt, knowing we were so close to getting that green card. So close to the doors opening. So close to freedom. It was as if we were trapped inside the walls of a city that was crumbling down all around us, desperately trying to find an escape route to safety. The green card was it.

The only worry I had about the final interview was that I had not answered one of their many questions 100 percent truthfully, and I wondered if I had been busted. It was the question that asked, "Has there ever been any mental illness in your family?" I knew damn well there had been mental illness in my family, Mom's crazy brother Noel, for one, but on the advice of my mother, I had answered no. I was worried that the authorities might have dug up some old records of my uncle's stint in the US Army, where he had been dishonorably discharged because of the many ludicrous things he had done, like frequently going AWOL.

This was the uncle who, at five years old, had seen his father ambushed and shot down in the streets of Dublin during the civil war in 1922. As I have said before, I don't think he ever fully recovered from that tragedy, and maybe that's why he was always a bit odd. Anyway, he was Mom's half brother, so she reassured me that the mental illness came from the side of the family I was not related to. If the embassy asked any questions, that was my story and I was sticking to it. Believe me, we had come too far in the process to blow it.

The interview went very well, and I realized they really couldn't have cared less about mental illness in the family and had no interest whatsoever in my crazy uncle. They had figured out the four of us in the immediate family were all quite sane, and that's all that mattered. We were welcomed to America. *What a great feeling!* The doors had been opened, and we could walk straight through.

However, it's never that simple—there always seems to be one more hurdle to jump over. And for us it was a huge hurdle. Before you could be admitted into the country, you had to prove to the US government that you were financially viable and would not become a burden to society. This meant you had to produce proof that you had a bank account in the United States that had at least ten thousand dollars in it. *Oh No!* We didn't have a US bank account with one dollar in it, much less ten thousand dollars. After all, it was against the law in Jamaica, and Tony, being his father's son and a faithful officer of the court, had never broken this law. I guess the United States didn't care about Jamaican laws, or Tony's loyalty to his profession. All I knew was that before we could actually pick up our green card, we had to find ten thousand US dollars. This was a serious problem.

Many of our friends were experiencing the same challenges that we were as they applied for their green cards. One of these friends was my husband's best buddy and sailing partner, William (the one who went to the Olympics with him in 1968). William was also married with two young children, and over the years our two families had grown very close. In fact, we had all decided that if and when we ever got our green cards, we were going to move to the same city together, wherever that might be. At least we would have one friend to lean on when things got tough, and we knew that starting all over again would be tough.

Tony was paranoid about smuggling money out of Jamaica, but we had to get ours out somehow. The government had already decreed that if you were caught smuggling money out of the island it would freeze your bank accounts and appropriate any monies you had left in them. We stood to lose everything without access to our funds. We had sold our house in Manor Park, which we had only owned for one year, and moved back to Red Hills once again. There was a real-estate frenzy going on at this time, everyone was selling, mostly in preparation for leaving the island. Even though we made no profit on the sale, we felt lucky just to have a buyer. What this enabled us to do, though, was to have some cash in hand—now we just had to find a way to convert it to US dollars. Thank goodness William came to our rescue. He was a shrewed businessman and had also been planning his escape from Jamaica for a long time.

William had a friend who was the captain of an oil tanker that was refueling in Kingston Harbor. He asked the captain if we could pay for the fuel in Jamaican dollars, and when he got back to the States, he could pay us back in US dollars. The captain agreed to do this for a small fee. It was risky. Tony and I had never met this "friend," and my Dad had lost a lot of money on similar transactions when the "friend" absconded with all the funds, never to be seen again. But the risk was worth it. We each gave him ten thousand Jamaican dollars, and one month later, twenty thousand US dollars, less his fee, was deposited into William's bank account in the United States. Whew, what a relief. At least we knew we had enough money to put a down payment on a house, and we would not starve when we got to America.

Tony was quite impressed with this transaction. Technically, he didn't actually smuggle any money out of the country, so he convinced himself, *technically,* that he had not broken the law. Maybe we could find other ingenious ways of getting our hard-earned money out of the country without breaking the law. We did.

So now we had our coveted green cards and we had been given six months to take up residence in the United States. The first phase was over, we had plotted our escape, decided on a country (the best country in the world in my opinion), gotten accepted into the country, and all we had to do now was figure out how we were going to survive financially. The next big decision for us was, where do we go? My first choice was either Florida or California because I knew my eyeballs would never freeze there, and I love palm trees—I just love them. The problem was, both states would have demanded a US undergraduate degree, plus another three years of law school, which meant seven more years of school for Tony. I could not imagine us being able to survive for seven years without an income from Tony, much less the expense of two college degrees. So where to go?

William's wife, Tricia, had just come back from a trip to Houston, Texas, and told us how much she loved it. We looked into it and found that the requirements to practice law in Texas were reasonable. If you had been a lawyer in another country for at least seven years, you only needed a three-year law degree—the US undergraduate degree was waived. We figured we might be able to survive for three years, after all, I could go back to work while Tony was at law school, as I had done once before. I frequently remind him that I have put him through law school twice in one marriage.

Tony and I flew to Houston to check things out, and immediately we knew that this city was where we were meant to be. Texas was booming in 1977, and seemed abounding with opportunities. However, we did not know a single person in Houston. Fortunately, I had one contact. I had been the head of an international organization in Jamaica called Birthright, which helped destitute pregnant women and newborn babies. I had the name and phone number of the head of the same organization in Houston. I called her up. Her name was Marilyn. Marilyn was so warm and welcoming. She made us feel right at home, and we immediately became good friends. It turned out that her husband, Burney, also happened to be a lawyer. Not only that, Burney's best friend was the dean of the law school at University of Houston, and he was very helpful in getting Tony accepted into his first year of law school.

We knew positively that we had made the right choice about Houston. Not only had Tony found a great law school, but Houston was on the Gulf. It had water, and that meant it had sailing. Even though we would not be able to afford everything right away, the future looked promising. We headed back to Jamaica with concrete plans to make our new home Houston, Texas. William and Tricia agreed that was the right choice and promised to follow in about three months.

Even though the Jamaican government was taking away numerous personal freedoms, surprisingly, it was still allowing emigrating citizens to ship their personal belongings out of the country. However, they were banned from taking any currency, so ingenious Jamaicans were coming up with all kinds of loopholes to smuggle their money out. We knew Manley and his cohorts would eventually take all our money if we left it there. Tony came up with a brilliant idea. He had an English client who needed to pay a large legal bill to Tony's law firm. Tony asked his permission to pay the bill for him in Jamaican dollars, and then the client could pay the money back to us in British pounds, which were easily convertible into US dollars. The client agreed, and just like that, we were able to get some more money out. Again, we were not really smuggling any money out of the country, so in Tony's mind, not really breaking the law. This was wonderful, especially as we knew Tony would not be working for three years, and we would be relying solely on my salary. Unfortunately, we did not get all our money out, but at least we had a jump start.

The day arrived for our final departure from our beautiful homeland. Many of our close friends had not left the country yet, and we all got together the night before to have a good cry and lots of hugs, not knowing when or if we would ever see each other again. The next morning, we had said good-bye to Tony's parents early, but his grandfather came to the airport to see us off. It was so sad to see the look on Iya's face, and he hugged Tony for a long time. This was probably the most difficult of the farewells. Iya's heart was breaking, and we knew it. We promised him we would do our best to come home for Christmas in only six short months. I think this was the only thing that kept Iya going.

The emotions were overwhelming at the airport. A myriad of feelings overtook me as I stood in the check-in line. Some of my dear friends and Mom were standing close by to give me moral support as feelings waxed and waned. At one moment I was angry because I felt we were being forced out of our homeland, but at the same time I was excited at the thought of a future in a safe and prosperous country. Then a mountain of fear would well up inside me as I wondered if I would ever get a job or how hard law school would be a second time around for Tony. *Would he make it?* I knew life would not be easy, but at least we would be safe, safe from communism and safe from ruthless crime. Mom was tearful, but she had made plans to come and visit us in a few weeks to help us get settled, and although she never mentioned it, I knew she was planning to check things out for herself. Her loneliness would be short lived.

We slowly made our way in the queue to the security checkpoint. I tried to appear at ease for the sake of our young children whose faces were full of apprehension and wonder at the same time. Our four year old son Sean was clinging to his cuddly brown teddy bear that almost never left his side. Just as we approached the final counter, a large security officer told my son to hand over his teddy bear. He did so cautiously, then watched in shock as the man took out a large knife and sliced the teddy bear open from head to toe in a violent manner. Poor Sean, he stood there in horror as stuffing went flying everywhere. I wanted so badly to shout at the man, "For God sake, was that really necessary" but wisely I kept my mouth shut, Sean started to cry and Michael's grip on my hand got tighter and tighter. Of course the guards were hoping to find U.S. dollars stuffed inside the innocent bear so they could apprehend us, but all they got was fluff. I reassured Sean that I would buy him a new teddy bear as soon as we got to America, but it was of little comfort. I know it was a sign of the times, but what a traumatic finale to our already stressed filled departure.

As the plane took off, with my two small children and my husband beside me, I looked down at the crystal-blue waters and white, sandy beaches of the small cays surrounding Kingston Harbor, and I was overcome with sadness. We had often sailed to those uninhabited cays, Lime Cay in particular, spending many joyful days there fishing for lobsters, mesmerized by the beauty of the tropical fish on the reef surrounding the tiny island. Those days of carefree weekends when we could enjoy the beauty of our birthplace, were now a thing of the past. I felt that from here on out, it was all going to be uphill—no more leisure time, just hard work—at least for a long while. I had to remind myself that, yes, we were losing our Caribbean lifestyle, but we were regaining a sense of belonging and a quality of life that we had lost in Jamaica. People in Houston were very friendly, and we already felt welcome—at least on our first visit no one had spat at us or thrown stones at our car and told us to go home.

An interesting thing happened as I was going through those nostalgic emotions. I overheard the conversation between a middle-aged black father and his children who were seated in the row in front of me in the plane. The father was dressed in an old but clean brown suit with a worn black tie and scruffy, but polished, black shoes. His children were in their finest Sunday clothes as well, old and well worn, but crisp and clean. He was obviously embarking on the same journey we were, immigrating to America in search of a better life for his children. He had no wife with him, and he struck me as probably being from the country. Country people in Jamaica have a different aura about them. They are softer and less aggressive than city people, hard-working and friendly. Life has value in the country, unlike the city. The man spoke in a gentle voice to his children, and what he said struck such a chord in me.

He told them, "Alright, unnu mus remember, we are goin to a white man's country now, han every day you will know it, han every day you will feel it, but it will be okay, we will prospa."

Wow, here were two Jamaican families, one white and one black, leaving their homeland for the same reason—in search of a better life—but each one anticipating a different welcome on the other side. I am sure this middle-aged black Jamaican had a lot more trepidation in his heart about his decision to leave his native land. At least in Jamaica, he would always have a sense of belonging no matter how bad things got, after all, he was black. He was now going to go to a land where he was not sure if he or his children would find that same sense of belonging, at least not for a while. He knew prejudices lay ahead, but in spite of it, he was willing to take the risk for his children. It was strange, but I knew exactly how this man felt. I had experienced it. The difference was, I was leaving those fears and prejudices behind, and he was just starting to embrace them. But we knew we would both "prospa."

It struck me how difficult it was for all Jamaicans, black or white, Chinese or Indian, rich or poor, to make the decision to leave their homeland, as it must be for anyone from any country. And yet so many did leave. I don't think Jamaica has yet recovered from the huge brain drain that occurred during the '70s and '80s. Not only did the majority of the educated professionals leave, but large numbers of hardworking honest people from all walks of society went searching for a better life. Jamaica lost some of its best citizens during those years. Damn that Michael Manley for breaking the backbone of the country and forcing so many productive Jamaicans out of their native land. I believe that if he had promoted healing, not hatred, and if he had not pursued his corrupt socialist agenda, Jamaica would be a very different country today.

However, we were the fortunate ones. We had been given a unique chance to go down a different path, a more stable path. Our journey was just beginning, and we could not look back. We just had to keep marching forward.

Pristine Beach
Photo©Cookie Kinkead

Spectacular Waterfalls
Photo©Cookie Kinkead

Majestic Mountains
Photo©Cookie Kinkead

Meandering Coastline
Photo©Cookie Kinkead

Famous Dunns River Falls

"In spite of the challenging conditions that corrupt politicians and violent criminals continue to create in our cities and countries around the globe, I will always remember, the world, especially Jamaica, is still full of magnificent beauty. It was hard to leave Jamaica's beauty" The author

CHAPTER 24

Safety in Texas, but terror in Jamaica

Houston was everything I had thought it was going to be. The first thing I noticed after a few days of living in America was that the muscles in my shoulders started to soften, and the tension I had been living with for so long, slowly left my body. I had gotten so used to the stress of living in Jamaica that my muscles had forgotten how to loosen up. When they relearned their normal relaxed position, it was a wonderful feeling.

One of the many visuals that struck me about Houston was the lack of burglar bars on windows and fences or walls around houses. The open access from the street to the front door gave me such a feeling of freedom. Obviously, people had no need to protect themselves the way we had to in Jamaica. Crime was practically nonexistent in our area. I developed such a sense of security that many times I forgot to lock my own front door.

I can't tell you how comforting it was to feel safe—a huge weight had been lifted from me. Another strange phenomenon happened after I started to relax. I discovered bundles of newfound energy and enthusiasm to enjoy the fun side of life. I guess all that energy was being absorbed up by fear and stress in Jamaica, and now it was all being released.

And, oh my goodness, the shops! They were everywhere and chockablock full with supplies. Every shelf was stocked to the brim with such a variety of groceries; I could buy all the tampons and cereal I wanted! There were apples, pears, peaches, plums, and fruits of all descriptions that we hadn't eaten in years. There were cookies and chocolates and choices of canned goods and snacks I had never seen before. There were fresh meats—steaks, lamb, and pork, not just goat and chicken. Each time I went to the supermarket, I was like a kid in a candy store. I think that feeling lasted for about a year before I finally got used to the fact that it would not change—food would always be on the shelves. I think most Americans just take abundance for granted, but I know that is not how it is in a lot of countries, and I will always appreciate a fully stocked supermarket.

We tried to buy a house but found out that when you don't have a job, no bank is eager to lend you money. We had the down payment, and we could make the monthly payments, but no lenders were keen on giving a mortgage to a student. Our fabulous new friend, Burney, came to the rescue and told us he would guarantee the loan until Tony finished school. Burney was a lifesaver, and we were able to buy a cute little four-bedroom home right beside one of the best Catholic grade schools in Houston. Our house had no fence, no gate, and no burglar bars.

Tony started law school within two weeks of our landing in Houston and was gone for fourteen hours a day, so I was pretty much alone. I missed my social network of friends terribly. I missed being able to pop in and visit whenever I wanted to and have a good old chat with a caring friend to empathize with me about whatever. For those first few weeks, I had no one to talk to, and I was very lonely. I missed my mother the most. In Jamaica she had been my rock.

I knew I had to find a job, but if I went back to computer programming, my children would not see either parent for most of the day. So the first job I took in Houston was delivering the *Yellow Pages*. It was very humbling and hard work hauling those heavy books up flights of stairs and going from house to house for hours, dropping the books at the doorsteps. Quite honestly, I was not used to such manual labor. In fact, I had never really done any manual labor in my life before that, and I hated it.

When the *Yellow Pages* gig was over, I took a job working in a day care center. I knew I could take my four-year-old to work with me there, so it seemed like a good idea. Again, I hated it, but we needed the money, and I did it. I was beginning to think Iya was right. With the little bit of money we did get out of Jamaica being used up very quickly on the house, Tony not earning a dime, and my not being able to take on a full time job because of the kids, I thought we were doomed to poverty.

Then, just when I was bemoaning that I had no one to commiserate with, Mom came up to visit. This was a huge comfort to me. With Tony away at law school fourteen hours a day and the deep void I was feeling from the loss of my friends, I was desperately lonely. I knew she could relate to my feelings, after all, she had been exactly there twenty-six years earlier.

Her visit meant the world to me. I wanted to show off our new city. I took her to the rodeo, the amusement park, the ice skating rink in the Galleria, the Space Center, and the Hyatt Regency with their revolving downtown restaurant, everywhere I could think of that would awe her. We were truly having fun until we got a phone call from Jamaica that threw us both into shock.

Dad had been coming home from his usual night at the golf club. As he was trying to get his key in the front door, three men grabbed him by the back of his collar and one pushed a loaded gun up to his temple. The man with the gun was angry (which is never good). He kept yelling, "White blood goin' to flow tonight." He told Dad to open the door, and he and his two cohorts pushed their way inside. "A goin' blow yu white brains all over di wall tonight," he kept shouting as they pushed my father forward. The man was holding the back of his collar so tight that Dad was choking. The pressure of the cold end of the loaded gun against his temple paralyzed him. They started yelling obscenities about "di white man" being the cause of their slavery, and they kept saying they were going to "blow his white head off."

Dad had always had the gift of the gab. Without ever kissing the Blarney Stone, he was full of blarney. I think this ability to sweet talk anybody saved his life that night. Even though I am sure he was scared out of his mind, somehow he did not panic. He started to talk in a quiet, calm voice, telling the men that he really had nothing at all to do with their slavery. In fact, he was Irish, and the Irish were also sent to Jamaica as slaves back in the day, (more like indentured servants but "slaves" worked better in this situation).

This was actually true, but the problem was, the Irish were not as strong as the Africans and most died of heat exhaustion and disease. But the "gun men" did not care that he was Irish; he was white, and to them he was the oppressor. They were determined to kill him. He had lost five close friends to murder in the last year, so he knew this was a serious situation, and he could die at any moment.

I can't imagine how terrorizing this must have been for him. His hair actually turned white within a few months after this incident, so I know his entire body went into shock. I kept thinking, as I was hearing the story, how fortunate we were that we had gotten out of the country when we did; we had left that very house just a few short weeks before. It was also miraculous timing that my mother was up visiting me when the gun men came. I am 100 percent certain, if we had been there, Mom and I would have been raped, and we would all have been murdered that night. Thank God, we were safe, and Dad only had to worry about saving his own life—that was hard enough. There was nothing of great value in the house, as my father was one of the most non-materialistic men I have ever known. Material possessions mattered so little to him that I actually witnessed him spraying his only pair of dress shoes black for Bridget's wedding in lieu of buying a new pair. Not because he was cheap, but because he just didn't care.

However, he did own one thing of value, a Rolex watch my brother Peter had given him for his fiftieth birthday. I know people have been murdered for their Rolex watches, and, ironically, this time a Rolex watch helped save his life. He slowly took the watch off his wrist and showed it to the men. He explained that it was a very expensive watch, and they could get a lot of money for it. They started to calm down as they examined the watch. He continued talking to them in a very quiet tone, telling them that he ran a canning factory that employed over one thousand "baby mothers." That was a common term for women in Jamaica. He told the men that if he did not show up for work the next day, the factory would close, and one thousand "baby mothers" would be out of work. They would all come looking for whoever was responsible for that. If the men killed him, they had better watch out, because Jamaica is a small place and people talk. It would not be his fault, but he knew the vengeance of one thousand "baby mothers" would eventually reach them.

Miraculously all the blarney worked, and the would-be killers took his advice and decided not to shoot him. However, they locked him up in the bathroom and proceeded to steal every single item in the house. They took everything their truck would hold: my mother's jewelry, the china, the cutlery, the linens, the TV, the stereo, and even the fridge. It took them about two hours, and I am sure those were the longest two hours of Dad's life, constantly wondering, as he heard them rummaging around outside, if they would change their minds and open the bathroom door and just start firing. I am guessing Dad prayed a lot that night. I know I would have been praying like hell. He was probably promising God all kinds of reparations that he could never fulfill, and knowing Dad, asking God for forgiveness for his wild ways.

Maybe his prayers were answered, maybe it was just luck, maybe it was his gift of the gab, maybe it was the Rolex watch, but somehow, his life was spared. In fact, he had done such a good job of befriending those men that when they had finished cleaning out the house, they knocked on the bathroom door and told him they were leaving his car keys on the floor. As they left, their exact words were, "Wi gone now, sah. Goodnight." He really had a way with people, and it sure helped him that night. They had taken everything, and, of course, he had no insurance, but that didn't matter; all that mattered was they did not take his life. He was very shaken up by this whole incident, and when he managed to get out of the bathroom, he walked out of his house that night and never ever returned. Mom and I were totally traumatized as we listened to the story.

Shortly after that, Dad sold our precious family home for little or nothing. Knowing him, he did not even consult Mom about it. But he didn't care, he just wanted to get rid of it; the burglary and attempt on his life were just too painful. He did not want to take the chance of it happening again. When Mom returned to Jamaica from her visit to Houston, her beautiful tropical home on the hillside was removed from her life. I know she felt a huge void. But even though there were thirty years of memories in that house, some very sad, some very joyful, she knew it was time to sell. Dad had done the right thing. She moved in with him into the small apartment he had rented in a busy residential neighborhood in town. It was a big adjustment for her, and deep down, she knew it was the beginning of the end of her life in Jamaica. At least she felt a bit safer in the apartment, but that too would be short lived.

Tom's canning factory 1964

CHAPTER 25

His heart literally broke from sadness

Mom had loved her visit to Houston; she loved everything about America. She loved the abundance in the stores, the variety of foods, the competence of employees, and the ease and speed by which things got done, but most of all, she loved feeling safe. When she returned to Jamaica, she was bound and determined to plan an exit strategy for herself to immigrate to America. The attempted murder on my Dad's life gave her the perfect opportunity to convince him it was not safe for her to live in Jamaica anymore. She could use this excuse to get him to apply for their green cards. She knew as long as Dad was working, he would have to stay in Jamaica, but she wanted out. She made her plans to move to Houston, and this time, if she played her cards right, she would have his blessing and full financial support, unlike the London experience. Dad was not an officer of the court as Tony had been, so he had no problems smuggling his money out of Jamaica. He had been slowly building up a stash of US dollars, waiting for the chance to smuggle them out. This could be a win-win situation for Mom. So she started plotting and planning her escape, something she was very good at by this stage.

Tony and I had made a promise to Iya, Tony's grandfather, that we would try to return to Jamaica for Christmas that first year. We still had money in Jamaica we could use to purchase the airline tickets as our bank account had never been frozen. This left us spending money while we were there, and we did not have to use any of our precious US dollars. We felt we might as well use up the Jamaican dollars because they could not be spent anywhere else. As the money devalued over the years, we ended up calling it "Monopoly money" because it was of no real value after a while.

The Jamaican Christmas vacation was wonderful. We stayed with Mike and Christine in Tony's old family house way up in the mountains of Stony Hill. Tony and I were able to enjoy our visit, knowing we had the safety net of our return tickets to the United States if we had to get out in a hurry. It was so exciting to see so many of our close friends again. I talked so much, my jaw almost locked. After all, I had six months of catching up to do.

It was great to see the family too. Tony's stepmother Christine prepared her traditional Christmas dinner of turkey, rice and beans, and plantains. Mom and Dad were also invited, and everyone, especially Iya, was thrilled to see us. We all enjoyed Christmas Day. Tony and I had planned to return to Houston on December 28, and as we were getting closer and closer to that date, we started to notice Iya getting more and more anxious. He missed Tony and his great-grandsons very much. Such a sensitive, emotional man was still convinced that Tony would be sweeping American streets for a living and that we were heading for financial ruin. This was a great worry to him. Then the unthinkable happened.

The day before we were to leave, Iya had worked himself up into such a state that he had a heart attack and died, right there at home, in the middle of the driveway. We were devastated. *What had we done to this poor old man?* His heart had literally broken from sadness and worry. That was truly difficult for Tony to handle. Convinced we had made the right decision to leave Jamaica, we did not realize what a toll it would have on the family. This was a tough one to bear. We buried Iya with deep sorrow and guilt, returning to Houston with heavy hearts.

CHAPTER 26

America . . . the greatest country in the world

The first two and a half years in Houston while Tony was in law school were quite difficult for us financially. I did get an accounting job, which paid the bills but no more. We were always short of money and could not afford to go out much, but all that did not seem to matter. We were safe, we had made many friends, and we knew Tony would one day graduate, although it seemed like an eternity away.

Tony's dedication and hard work meant he was in the top 2 percent of his class, on the Law Review, and well on his way to graduating summa cum laude. We were hopeful he could land a decent job with those impressive credentials.

The wonderful thing about America is that if you are willing to work hard, there is great opportunity. We did have to start all over at the bottom rung of the ladder and crawl our way back up, but it was all worth it. Sure enough, when Tony did graduate, he was offered a job with one of Houston's best law firms. My parents and his parents all flew in for his graduation. It was not only a huge relief to us, but now all the parents, especially my mother, could rest a little easier knowing that our future looked hopeful. No sweeping streets, as Iya had predicted.

Tony's new job was fantastic. What an honor to work at such a prestigious law firm, which had over nine hundred attorneys worldwide. Tony worked in the international corporate department, and some wonderful people were in that group, many of whom are still good friends today. He worked long, hard hours but was rewarded with good friendships and fun times. Plus, the job had great potential (Dad was right after all!), and we started to earn real money. What a great feeling, and I was so relieved that finally the burden of earning all the household income was off my shoulders. Later on, when the children were older, I went back to university myself. At forty-seven, I graduated magna cum laude from the University of Houston, with a BA in accounting. It's never too late. Those two little letters after my name greatly improved my earning potential. Even though I would never earn as much as Tony, I know I would be able to support myself if I ever had to. Another lesson learned from my mother's mistakes.

Meanwhile, back in Jamaica, it was now 1980, and Prime Minister Manley decided to hold an election. By now the opposition party, the JLP, was determined to regain the leadership of the country, and it had pulled out all the fire power it had to do so. The night of the election Mom called me, scared out of her mind. She and Dad were hiding under her bed in their little apartment, and she told me bullets were literally flying through the windows as gangs roamed the streets, shooting off their guns wherever they felt like it.

It was a violent election, I am told that over eight hundred people died, but the JLP did win; Jamaica had a new leader, and a new political party came to power. Maybe, just maybe, the new prime minister, Eddie Seaga, could stop the communist march. I'd heard a rumor that if Michael Manley had won that election he would have been assassinated. I have no idea who wanted him dead. It could have been the CIA; it could have been the JLP; it could have been his own Marxists bad boys who seemed to have taken over or one of the dons he pissed off. Who knows? However, the rumor was quite believable, because all sense of civility had been lost in Jamaica by this time, and heinous crimes were being committed left, right, and center.

Before Tony and I had left the country, we had heard that the CIA had beefed up its staff in Jamaica, as the number of employees at the embassy had quadrupled. We had often attended social events that the American diplomats were also invited to. I remember one such social event quite vividly.

We were at a cocktail party at the magnificent old colonial hotel called Terra Nova. The Terra Nova was rich in history and ambiance, each room flanked by mahogany columns with gold trim, red velvet curtains pulled back from every window, and whirring fans in every room making futile attempts to keep the guests cool. It was a perfect setting for tropical espionage and intrigue.

I am not sure what got into me, whether I thought I was in the middle of a James Bond story or if I was just young and stupid, but I had noticed a lot of fresh new American faces, so I got curious. I walked up to one of the good-looking, crew-cut young men and asked him if he was a CIA agent sent down to Jamaica to save us from a Cuban fate. He actually turned ashen and stood there in astonishment as if he had been busted. I guess it was an inappropriate question, but I was curious and hopeful. Did I truly think he just might fill me in on the latest US plans to keep Jamaica from falling into communist hands? No, I just knew there had to be plans. Of course, he never answered me, but his reaction gave it away. A lot was going on behind the scenes everywhere, yet no one could prove anything, and gossip was always denied. Still, they have a saying in Jamaica, "If not suh it go, it almost suh it go," which means if a rumor was going around, and it was not exactly true, it was almost exactly true.

However, Jamaica now had a new leader, Edward Seaga. Maybe the CIA had had a plan after all, because Seaga was definitely not a communist. In fact, he immediately started reestablishing relationships with the Western first-world countries, like the United States and England. Ronald Reagan came to visit, and the Queen of England came to visit—very different from the heads of state who had visited under Michael Manley's reign. Seaga secured loans from the IMF (that Manley had declined) and did his best to help Jamaica recover from the almost-bankrupt state Manley had left. There was a new sense of hope floating around, but it was still not enough to change Mom's plans for escaping.

The problem was that so much corruption and civil unrest existed in the country; Seaga was fighting a huge uphill battle. What was happening, from my observation, was that during this time and throughout the '80s, the politicians were losing control of the very garrison neighborhoods they had created. These armed gangs were now growing, and they were morphing from political gangs into organized-crime drug gangs. These drug gangs were led by dangerous crime lords or dons. The dons brought more and more guns into the island and gradually started gaining control over the politicians, the businessmen, and the entire community. Instead of the politicians ruling the gangs, the gangs started ruling the politicians. Extortion, blackmail, and protection rackets were common. Everyone was afraid of getting on the wrong side of these dons—who could have you blown away for as little as twenty dollars. My island home had become one of the scariest places in the world to live, and all I kept thinking was, *My mother is still there.*

Although much of the violence in Kingston had taken place in the poverty-stricken neighborhoods, it was rapidly spreading everywhere. No one living in Kingston, rich, poor, black, or white, could escape the unrest and pervasive lawlessness. It was like living life on a roulette wheel, spinning round and around, not knowing if today was the day the ball would land on your number, and *you* would face the terror. For Mom, it was harrowing, especially after what my father had been through. The long wait for the illusive little three-inch by two-inch green card (which is actually pale blue) was excruciating. But this card was the only thing that gave you the legal "right of abode" in the United States; it was the ticket to freedom and the most precious possession you could have in Jamaica at the time. Everyone wanted it. The waiting period was painfully slow, and with each day came more and more frustration, knowing time was running out. It was a miracle that Mom managed to escape the violence unscathed during those tense years of the late '70s and early '80s. Unfortunately, this was not the case for Tony's family.

Houston—Cathy (Tony's sister) Ena, Michael and Sean—1980

CHAPTER 27

For those left behind . . . life in Jamaica took on the flavor of a horror movie

Even though many people had fled Jamaica, I always felt desperately worried for those left behind on the troubled island, especially Mom and Tony's stepmother, Christine. Christine's family had been in Jamaica for hundreds of years, and later, she told us that during the '80s, when everyone left, she had felt a tremendous sense of loss and bewilderment. She said she knew she was still living in her own country, the country her father, grandfather, and great-grandfathers were all born in, the country her ancestors had helped shape by becoming merchants, traders, legislators, lawyers, and farmers. Her relatives never had a lot of money but always felt complete because they always had the security of family and friends nearby.

But all that had changed, and she barely recognized her country. Christine had not only lost all her immediate family and most of her friends to migration, but in the space of two years, she had lost nine different doctors who left for foreign lands. She told me she used to mourn Jamaica losing so many of its young people.

"The movers, the doers, the creators, and the contributors to society are now making their impact elsewhere" she had said. "A great gap has been created in Jamaican society that will never be filled." Everything around her had changed—the society she had grown up in was gone and now living in Houston, London, Toronto, New York, Miami, and various other parts of the world, causing a huge void in her life.

Without her network of friends and family, her sense of security was gone—her sense of belonging was gone. Finally, her youngest daughter Cathy also left the country. Afterward, Christine told me it hit her that if she and her husband suddenly died, no one in Jamaica would even notice they were missing for perhaps a week or more.

She had to learn to cope with it though, because Tony's father, Mike, had no intention of leaving Jamaica, and, unlike my father, never even considered applying for a green card. Mike was in his late fifties and had no money outside of the island, and he knew he could not start over at this stage. Christine realized her fate was sealed, but she did not know her life was about to take on the flavor of a horror movie.

It started one day when a stranger walked into Mike's office and told him he had been hired to kill him. *What? How could this be true?*

Later, when Mike phoned Tony to tell him, Tony's reaction was, "Can you repeat that?" If the man was serious, why was he standing in Mike's office, unarmed and looking so remorseful? A real assassin would have already blown Mike away. However, unbelievable as it seemed, it was true.

The story goes that a former law partner had been suspected of embezzling millions of dollars from the law firm, and Mike had been trying to gather enough evidence to have the man prosecuted. The first thing happened after Mike announced his intentions: a fire broke out in his building. And guess where it started? That's right, in the former law partner's office, where all the evidential accounting files were stored. It was determined the fire was arson because traces of gasoline were found. Although no one could prove who set the fire, who else would have had a motive? So Mike had to dig deeper and deeper to find more evidence to have the crook locked away. I don't know if he was getting close, but I guess the ex-partner decided the only way to get rid of the investigation was to get rid of Michael Nunes, and that's exactly what he tried to do.

On the day the man showed up in Mike's office, he stood there unfolding a story that seemed to come straight out of a Hollywood script.

"Mi been hired to kill yu suh," he calmly told Mike. "Mi suppose to run yu off di hillside or off di road to make it look like han occident."

Mike just sat there and listened without reaction.

"Mi been following yu for three months now," the man continued, "han mi decided mi can't kill a man dat go to church on Sundays."

Then the man showed Mike his passport and a ticket to Panama where he was supposed to go immediately after he had successfully completed the hit. I believe he thought Mike Nunes would pay him more money *not* to kill him than the ex-partner had paid him to kill him, but he did not know who he was dealing with.

Not only did Mike not offer him any more money, he quietly picked up the phone, called the police, and immediately had the man arrested. Another reason the hired hit man may have decided to come clean was that Jamaicans can be very superstitious, and perhaps he thought if he killed a man who went to church every Sunday, a curse would be put on him. Who knows, but fortunately for Mike, the man could not go through with his plans.

However, this new death threat was very disturbing to all of us, but especially to Tony's poor stepmother. This automatically increased her anxiety tenfold. It was all quite terrorizing. How could we keep him safe if he would not leave the country? And how could he keep himself safe amidst these personal death threats, much less the random violence that was permeating everywhere? For a brief time he did agree to hire a so-called "body guard," but that was short lived as he declared the bodyguard was more trouble than he was worth. Everyone's nerves were on edge.

Mike and Christine lived in a house way up in the Blue Mountains in a place called Stoney Hill. It took about forty-five minutes to drive there from Kingston, but the drive was worth it once you saw the spectacular view of the city from every angle of the house. The access dirt road was full of twists and turns, and the house was so remote that no telephone lines had ever been installed. The closest neighbor was a quarter of a mile away. The couple had lived there for twenty-five happy years, watching their children grow and enjoying the many memories of good times spent with friends. However, in the early 1980s, the only member of their family still at home was Cathy, their teenage daughter.

Shortly after the foiled assassination attempt on Mike's life, Christine noticed three men stalking their house. At first, she only saw them on the perimeter of the garden, and she began to notice missing items, such as a wheelbarrow and ladders. Then one night, a boyfriend of Cathy's was visiting the house, and while they were outside saying good-bye, Christine heard a terrorizing scream from Cathy. She and Mike ran outside to find two men holding a knife to Cathy's throat and demanding money. Mike started to fight off the men, hitting them over the head with the only weapon in his hand, which was his dressing gown. Not very effective, however, it startled the men so much that they let Cathy go, and a wild chase took place all through the house.

In the mêlée, one of the men managed to stab Cathy's boyfriend, and blood started spilling everywhere. I guess adrenalin kicks in when you are faced with this kind of assault, and you do crazy things, but Christine says when she saw all the blood, she went into the kitchen and got a mop and started to mop it up, fighting off the invaders with the mop if they got close to her. I think it was a lucky thing that the invaders only had a knife, because if they'd had a gun, things would have turned out very differently. They eventually demanded the keys to Christine's car, which she wisely handed over, and they took off. The boyfriend survived the attack, thank goodness, but Christine never saw her car again, and the worst was yet to come.

A week later, Christine and Mike came home to find their dog dead with a machete slash along his side. Shortly after that, their housekeeper was gun-butted when an intruder came through the open back door demanding money. Then their gardener was shot in the neck when he surprised two men roaming outside the house at seven in the morning. The gardener lived, but night after night the family was awakened by gunfire in the area. Their nearest neighbor was held up and beaten, and he and his wife were tied up and robbed. Their neighborhood was being terrorized, and so were they.

There were so many nightmarish incidences that the neighbors all got together and formed a "neighborhood watch." This meant that the men who owned guns would patrol each evening, carrying VHF radios that were linked to the police station and patrol cars. Christine became a radio addict. She says she carried her radio everywhere and never felt safe without it. Unfortunately, the VHS radio only gave her a false sense of security, because no number of radios could protect her from what was to come.

The first incident happened one afternoon as my stepmother went into her kitchen to start cooking dinner. Alone at home, she suddenly sensed someone outside, but she could not pinpoint the feeling. She walked out of the kitchen and down the passageway toward her bedroom where she again heard a noise of someone outside. I will share with you what happened next in her exact words.

I walked into my bedroom, and there at the window, standing on a ladder or some such, was a man.

"Whatever are you doing here?" I demanded.

"A come to kill yu, yu white bitch!" he replied to me. My heart started pounding. I drew back into the passage, out of his sight, and then into my study, which was right beside the bedroom, and got on both my radios. I had a CB and a marine-band VHF. I called my husband Mike on the CB, but as usual, he had not turned the radio on. I called the police on that circuit also, but they did not answer. Then I called the coastguard on the VHF, and they called the police on their direct radio link. Someone from Portmore, twenty-five miles away, answered my call for the police, but they told me they did not know where my house was and could not come.

By this time, I discovered that the man outside had turned off the electricity at the mains but had only turned off one circuit, so I still had power for the radios but no electricity for lights, and it was getting dark. I began to fear that Mike would come home, find the lights out, and think it was just another power cut (which are frequent in Jamaica). Then he would get out of the car without fear, and the man would kill him. I called and called on the CB radio, but he still did not answer. Then I heard a great banging on the kitchen door. I put on a pair of shoes and fled through my study door to my nearest neighbor, who lived a quarter of a mile away. Only the young son Claude, who was about nineteen years old, was home. We got flashlights, and he grabbed a machete, and we returned to the house just in time to meet Mike driving up our driveway. So we three joined forces, and Michael and I and Claude started to chase the man who was inside the house at this point. The house was open, the kitchen door had been broken down, and the stove (on which the supper had been cooking) had been turned off. Nothing was apparently missing, but the man was still roaming around the house. We could not capture him, and he simply would not leave. Eventually, I took down the fire extinguisher from the kitchen wall and gave it to Claude. He came face to face with the man round a corner, and fired off the extinguisher at him, covering him with foam. At that, finally the intruder left, but I never felt safe in that house again.

The petty thefts and vandalism went on for some time in the neighborhood. Nightly, we heard on the radio of houses being broken into. One of the Neighborhood Watch patrol had been shot. A housekeeper left at home with two small children was held up and raped. In my quiet mountaintop home, I had become part of a garrison community, where vigilantes walked with guns, and the women stayed home with the children, listened to the VHF radio, and prayed for the safety of their men. I got so upset that Mike finally consented to put the house up for sale.

Even after all that had happened, Mike knew he would never leave his homeland. Christine begged him to at least sell the remote house and move closer to Kingston. He begrudgingly agreed, but that was the only change he was willing to make.

CHAPTER 28

Houston here I come . . .
for mom life couldn't be sweeter

With the ever-increasing terrorizing stories that Mom heard every day, especially what was happening to her friend Christine up in Stony Hill, she was beginning to think her chances of escaping before becoming a victim to crime were getting slimmer and slimmer. After all, at that time, being white in Jamaica was like having a big red target on your back.

Then one day, she went to the mailbox, and there it was—the precious letter with the US Embassy seal. She immediately called my brother Peter and me to give us the good news, and a collective sigh of relief rippled through our family. Peter had married and moved to Vancouver, Canada, I was in Houston, and all of Tony's siblings, except the youngest sister Cathy, had emigrated to England or the United States. The younger generation had moved on to safety, but our parents had not. This was Mom's opportunity. The escape route she had been plotting and waiting for now lay in front of her. On that memorable day, Mom's life changed forever. She would once again be emigrating to a new country, but this time it was the United States of America, and this time it was all her choice. Even though Dad was traveling with her, she knew he would return to Jamaica. She knew for sure he was never going to give up his work, and by now she had finally accepted the fact that he was never going to give up his lifestyle of rum, women, and reggae, no matter the risks.

As soon as she could, Mom high tailed it out of Kingston and arrived on my doorstep in Houston. With the money Dad had smuggled out of Jamaica, he was able to purchase a two-bedroom apartment for both of them (he claimed). However Mom convinced him that "for tax purposes" he needed to put the title solely in her name. *WOW! My mother was becoming quite savvy.* I'm not sure why Dad agreed to this, but he did. It was not a very big apartment, but it was cozy. He also opened a bank account "for tax purposes"—in her name. What a negotiator she had become. Then he bought a car in her name. *What was going on?* Quite honestly, I believe a lot of Dad's generosity stemmed from Catholic guilt, because he always compensated his family in financial ways to make up for his neglect in other areas. I guess it eased his conscience a bit, but he did not have to be that generous. Thank goodness, he was raised Catholic, as his guilt was a tremendous gift to my mother.

A few weeks after Dad got everything settled in Houston, he returned to work in Jamaica, alone, just as Mom had predicted. She knew she probably would not see him again for at least six months, and even then, only for a quick visit. Her plan was playing out just as she had hoped. Even though they were still married—and maybe, deep down, she still had some distant feelings for him—her brain had finally taken over and convinced her that the romance was dead. In her mind, the relationship was now just a business one, and she seemed to be the better business person. I do not think my father ever realized that he had been totally manipulated in Houston. But Mom had been paying close attention all those years in Jamaica, and he had taught her well.

Before he knew it, she had gotten everything she wanted, and without ever having to go to court. I know Dad still believed that she was madly in love with him (his ego could not have handled anything else), so he thought he was making those financial decisions as a couple. But unbeknownst to him, Mom had moved on. She had finally realized he was never going to change his ways, and she stopped letting it bother her. Emotionally, her relationship with him was over, so why make herself his enemy? She wisely chose to remain his friend, and it paid off.

Now, Mom was sitting pretty. *How could life get any sweeter?* She was legally living in the United States of America near her grandchildren, she had a roof over her head (that was all hers), money in the bank, and to top it off, she never had to worry about bullets flying through her apartment window at night. Sure, she may not have gotten to this place without financial support from her husband, but so what? In my opinion, he owed her. She had given him the best years of her youth, and it was the least he could do after the torment he had put her through. No matter how she got there, the most important thing was that Mom had finally landed securely on her feet, exactly where she wanted to be. I was so proud of her, especially since she had come from a generation where husbands had the majority of the power in a marriage. In her own way, she had learned how to make the leap into the liberated generation and to accept the notion of an independent future. Mom was in her early fifties now, but she was just beginning a brand-new phase of her life, and she never wanted to look back. Her life in that "that godforsaken place" was finally over.

Not only had Mom successfully escaped a painful, dysfunctional marriage by moving to Houston, but miraculously, she had also escaped unscathed from Jamaica's reign of terror. For Maeve O'Brien, it was a joyous time.

Houston—Christmas morning 1997

161

CHAPTER 29

Back in Jamaica the worst ordeal was yet to come

The huge relief we all felt when Mom got out of Jamaica unharmed was overshadowed by the scary knowledge that there were other members of the family still there. In our early years of living in Houston, our conversation was often about the terrible crimes and conditions that existed in Kingston. It was fresh in our minds, especially for Mom, and she became deeply worried about Christine and Mike. She had every right to be worried, as their worst ordeal was still to come.

The childhood home of the Nunes family finally sold, and Christine and Mike were scheduled to move out in a couple of days when the most terrorizing of all incidents occurred. Again, I will put it in Christine's own words.

I picked up Mike at the airport as he had been on a business trip to Miami. I asked him if he would consider spending the night with a friend (whom I had stayed with while he was away) as I was scared to sleep in the house where I had spent so many years. But he pooh-poohed my fears and told me he wished to go home, for he was tired.

We went straight to bed, and he went off to sleep. I was awake and reading for a while, and then I, too, turned off my light and drifted off to sleep. At about midnight, our Alsatian dog barked and woke us. We got up and checked outside the house, but could see nothing. We went back to bed, and Mike went back to sleep, but I could not sleep. Suddenly, a light shone in the room and, startled, I opened my eyes. At first I thought it was a firefly, which gives off a bright light. Then I realized it was coming from the window, from a flashlight held by a man who was standing on a ladder

(I guessed). I lay paralyzed—for several hours, it seemed to me, although I know it was only for seconds.

Then I saw a gun come through the window, and I thought: What am I going to do? Is this really happening? Surely this is a bad dream. *But it was real enough. Next I thought,* How can I save Mike?

I rolled off my side of the bed, which was away from the window, to my Neighborhood Watch radio, which I kept on the floor next to my bed. I started screaming, hoping Mike would wake up and roll off the bed and take shelter from the gun, but it was not to be. As he woke from his exhausted sleep, he turned toward me, and as he turned over, there was a loud explosion, and Mike said, "He's got me!"

I grabbed the radio and called "Stony Hill base, Stony Hill base!" which was the call sign for the police. Immediately, Sergeant McInnes in his police car answered me, and I told him what had happened. I learned afterward that Sergeant McInnes was about ten miles away when he got the call and had a long drive before he could get to us.

I also learned afterward that nearly everyone on the Neighborhood Watch radio system was listening to me as I related what happened, and that three of the neighbors came carefully along the dirt road leading to our house, to watch and wait until the police arrived, which they did in about fifteen minutes. The first I knew that rescue had come was when the men outside the window disappeared. They had been standing there all the time, threatening me, and asking me for money, jewelry, and cameras. At one time, I was really terrified, for I heard the grill on the study next to our bedroom rattling, and I thought they had smashed the locks and were coming into the house to finish the job they had started. But they were just climbing the grill to cut the radio antennas, not realizing that the radio I was using was handheld and had its own antenna.

When the men disappeared, I rushed over to Mike, to find him bleeding from a wound in his stomach.

Shock, *I thought.* He will be suffering from shock. I must keep him warm and stop the bleeding. *So I grabbed a pillow and put it beside him to stop the bleeding; then I wrapped a blanket around him to hold the pillow in place. Finally, lights shone from the driveway into our bedroom as two cars drove up, and I heard the voice of one of our neighbors telling me that the police were here and asking me to let him into the house.*

Mike held on to me. "Remember that I love you," he told me. "If I don't make it, remember that."

"Darling, you will live," I assured him. "Don't worry!"

I called out to my rescuers and rushed into the study to open the door and let them in.

First in was a burly man with a long gun (I know nothing about guns) whom I recognized. He was followed by the police sergeant. They took one look at Mike and told me that he had to be taken to hospital right away. I was so glad I had wrapped him in a blanket. They picked him up in their arms and put him in the back of the police jeep and drove off. The police sergeant stayed with me and told me he would drive me to the hospital. I dressed and locked up the house as safely as I could. Then I left and went with the police sergeant to the University Hospital.

It was an hour's drive to the hospital. When I got to there, the sergeant took me into Casualty, where Mike was lying on a stretcher. Someone, I learned later, a doctor who lived in our neighborhood, had telephoned and alerted the duty team that someone with a stomach wound was coming in, and they would have to get ready to operate. I waited with Mike until they'd set up a drip, given him an injection, and taken him into the operating room. Dr Tulloch was the operating surgeon.

Tired, terrified, and in shock, I called my friend Anne Lake, who lived not too far from the hospital. She picked me up and brought me to her house where she fed me warm milk and sugary coffee and put me to bed after we had talked for a while. At about five thirty in the morning, I woke up and could not sleep anymore, so I began telephoning the family. First off, I telephoned my son Steve and then Tony and told them, and then I called Mike's partners, and finally I called my daughter Cathy. After that, all is a blur for the next three weeks.

When Tony got the phone call from Jamaica, I remember him saying, "Those bastards. I knew it was just a matter of time, damn them." He was angry, but instinctively sprang into his "duty calls" mode, as he knew Christine would need all the support she could get from the children, especially the eldest son. He got the next flight out of Houston. At the hospital, Tony met the head of the abdominal team, Dr. Mike Branday. As luck would have it, the doctor had been to school with Tony, so they knew each other well and could speak frankly. He had not been on duty that night but had taken over the next morning. He told Tony the surgery had gone well.

When Tony saw his dad lying on the bed in ICU, he wept. Mike was unconscious and looked like death. He was very pale. There were tubes sticking out everywhere, and a breathing tube was down his throat; drips of all kinds were going in and out of his body. It is always a very scary sight for the ordinary layman to walk up to a hospital bed and see such unfamiliar gadgets that doctors have attached to a loved one, knowing it must be okay but still feeling so helpless. As Tony looked around, he noticed the windows of the room were wide open, and flies were buzzing in and out. Concerns grew that his dad was not going to make it. He spoke to his friend Dr. Branday.

"I want to move to move him to Miami. I think he has a much better chance of survival there," Tony told the doctor.

Dr. Mike reassured Tony that there was less chance of infection right where he was. "Believe me, Tony, fresh air is much better than dirty air from air-conditioning ducts. That's how infections occur in the hospitals in America."

Tony had his doubts, but he had to believe him, after all, he was the expert. Dr. Mike told Tony that sixteen doctors had worked on his dad the night before, and they had done a great job. We learned later that his surgery was successful, but it was so complicated that it is now used as a case study to train young interns.

The bullet had gone in at an angle, through his intestines, through his spleen, through his lung, missed his heart by one inch, and exited out his back. He'd lost five pints of blood (which didn't seem possible), and they had to remove part of his intestines and his spleen. But the doctor assured Tony that Mike had a good chance of making it.

"Your father has a very strong heart," Dr. Mike told him. Tony felt better as he began to realize his dad was in very good hands.

That evening, details of the shooting were announced on television. Friends started to arrive at the hospital in droves to donate blood, and they were horrified when they heard what had happened. For days, Mike's progress was being updated on the evening news. It seemed that what had happened to this high-profile lawyer was quite shocking to a lot of people, and everyone wanted to know how he was doing. He became quite a newsworthy story.

Meanwhile, Tony and his brother and sisters, who had all arrived after hearing the news, went up to their childhood home every day to pack up the house so that Christine would not have to worry about anything except staying at the bedside of her husband. The nurses had told her that when she came to sit with him and held his hand, the heart monitor got much stronger. This was a great comfort to her, so she spent her days in the hospital while the kids packed boxes. How fortunate it was that they had sold the house prior to this horrendous incident. They had bought a much smaller townhouse in a gated community, which was going to be available within a few days.

While Tony was in Jamaica, he went to visit his father every day. His father had a respirator breathing for him, and he always had a look of anguish in his eyes. On around the third day, as Tony was looking at the pain on his father's face, Mike opened his eyes and weakly signaled that he wanted to write something. Tony gave him a piece of paper and a pen. He scribbled, "Just let me go, I want to die." The head nurse was in the room at the time, and she exploded. "What yu mean yu wan to die? Yu think we have worked on yu so hard to let yu die. Dere is no way we are goin' let yu die. Just stop dat foolishness!"

Tony looked down at his father. Mike had always been a fighter, and Tony knew he would fight this. Once the breathing tube was out and the pain subsided, Mike would survive.

Mike spent ten days in intensive care and two more weeks in a private room in the hospital. The amusing thing to us was that when he was discharged and received his bill, he complained bitterly at the cost. It was all of five hundred dollars. He thought that amount was outrageous, way too much money to spend for a hospital stay. It was a very good thing Tony had not brought him to the United States. We would still be paying his hospital bill. But this feistiness his dad displayed was a good sign. It showed us he was back to his old irritable self. Somehow he had beaten the odds and survived this terrible ordeal. He may have physically recovered, but I don't think that, emotionally, Christine ever has.

Christine continues her story.

We learned later that there had indeed been a contract put out on Mike's life, and suspicion fell heavily on the ex-partner who was being prosecuted. However, no one was ever brought to justice for the contract, although the authorities did capture one of the shooters that night, and he was given six years in jail.

It was a long time ago, yet even now there are nights when I do not sleep. I call them my "white nights," when I lay awake, toss and turn, and hear imaginary noises in the darkness of the night.

Mike went on to live for another ten years. I believe he would have lived much longer had his body not been put through such trauma from the shooting. He remained in his beloved Jamaica until the day he died. And, although in life he had gone through hell at times, he could not have asked for a more peaceful death. He went sailing one Sunday afternoon, as he often did, anchored the boat at his beloved Lime Cay, went for a little swim, climbed back onto the boat, and told Christine, "I have to lie down, I don't feel so well."

As he lay on the deck he whispered, "I am sorry to do this to you," and then a few moments later, he was dead. No sailor could ask for a better death.

He had a quiet death, which he deserved, but now poor Christine, at sixty years old, was left totally alone in a country that had become unbearable for her to live in. She had no money outside of the island, no green card, and her Jamaican dollars were devaluing rapidly. All her children were scattered, three in Houston, one in Miami, and one in England. Now she was really alone. What was she going to do?

Well she did what she had wanted to do for a long time. The exact same thing my mother had done, she applied for her green card—and waited.

CHAPTER 30

Just how many times can charm and blarney save dad's life?

It is still very painful to think about the terrorizing ordeals that Tony's father Mike and Christine experienced in their beloved homeland during the '80s. I am eternally grateful that neither Mom nor I had to live through such a nightmare. I believe we both got out just in time. I am 100 percent sure that if we had stayed in Jamaica, our whole family would have been murdered, especially after the violent break-in into our house in Red Hills just a couple of weeks after we had left. I truly believe our move to Houston was the best decision we ever made, and Mom's following us a few years later was the best decision she ever made.

Today, there are many Jamaicans of all walks of life and of all colors who are now living in various parts of the world, "making their contribution to their new countries instead of their beloved Jamaica," as Christine says. They left Jamaica for multiple reasons, but for the most part, because of the same reasons we did: political corruption, financial instability, and the terrifying crime wave that engulfed Jamaica during the '70s, '80s, and '90s. It was a disruptive and devastating time in Jamaica's history.

Although my anger is waning as the years go by, whenever I think about it, the feelings of resentment still surface. There are many memories I share with my fellow Jamaicans of the hardships of being forced out of the country of my birth, forced to uproot and move away, forced to start over with nothing, forced to lose all financial security, and forced to take great risks far away from the security of family and friends, and these memories are all painful. For our family though, in the long run, it was a very successful move. Mom, Tony and I, and the children found safety, security, and great opportunities in the United States of America, our new home. But not all Jamaican immigrants were as fortunate—we were some of the lucky ones, and for this we are eternally grateful.

Our anxieties were not over, however, and they would intensify whenever another terrorizing story would flow out of Jamaica. And there were many. Those we had left behind were still living in the midst of unrest and fear, and that was a constant worry to us. I was especially worried about Dad.

It was his choice of course, like Mike Nunes, to remain in his beloved Jamaica, even though there were constant reminders of the built-up anger and hatred toward white people at the time. Even though he had his green card, and even after surviving a few more brushes with death, surprisingly, Dad stayed.

One of these brushes with death came during the gas strikes in the '80s. There were fires, car jackings, murders, and ambushes all over the streets of Kingston as people started rioting because of the rising cost of fuel. It turned out that the people rioting and setting up road blocks were paid hooligans hired by the now-out-of-power communists. Of course, during the chaos that was taking place, all the sane people of Kingston stayed sheltered in place, in the safety of their homes, but not my fearless spirited father. He set off in the middle of the riots to drive across Kingston to visit his daughter Bridget, who was living there at the time. As he drove through the smoke-filled streets, his car was stopped and surrounded by an angry mob of men shouting, "White man mus' die." They started rocking the car back and forth as they tried to reach in and drag him out. My quick-thinking father saw his leather briefcase on the seat beside him and shouted to the men in his best patois, "No, man, I is a doctor, I'm on my way to save a life, yu haffi let mi go." At this, the mob stopped rocking his car and started shouting among themselves, "Im is a doctor, let im go, im is a doctor!" and at that, they opened a path for his car, and he drove off. I guess my father became a doctor that night, and his life was spared once again. But we were all beginning to question just how many times his charm and blarney would get him out of trouble, and just how many lives he had left. But he was the risk taker of the family, and it was ultimately his choice to remain in Jamaica. Mom and I chose to move on.

CHAPTER 31

"She's going straight to heaven and I'm going straight to hell"

Compared to Kingston, my mother's life in Houston was very peaceful. She never had to deal with angry mobs trying to drag her out of her car or bullets flying through her bedroom windows or racial slurs being hurled at her constantly. In fact, life became quite relaxing. She got involved in the church, doing her usual charitable work. Mom spent a lot of time with her grandchildren, who gave her great joy, especially our third son, Brian, who was born in Houston after she had moved there. She was very close to Brian, and she spent a lot of time with him from infancy right up to his teenage years. They had a special bond. Brian, who is our deep-thinking, spiritual child, misses his grandmother the most. He often tells me, "Grandma was around today, I felt her presence." I wish I could feel her, but I guess I am not spiritual enough.

In Houston, Mom made some friends but not many. Life was different. She never had the wide social network of friends she enjoyed in Jamaica. Her social life was mostly intertwined with my social life. She had no housekeeper, no gardener, and no cook. She had no "twin sister" just around the corner to confide in. I am sure she missed the few friends that were still left in Jamaica, but other than that, there was not much left there to miss, and whatever there was paled in comparison to what she gained.

And what she gained was priceless. She never had to worry about her husband not coming home for dinner or wonder what "lassie" he was with that night. In fact, she only saw him about twice a year, and even then she made him stay at my house during those visits.

She never had to worry about whether she would become the victim of a deliberate violent crime. Although I am well aware that the world is full of evil, damaged people, and that you can never completely escape crime no matter where you live, I know that in Houston she was a thousand times safer. And greatest gain of all, she never had to worry about money.

My father had moved enough money out of the island for them both to live on, anticipating the day he might also have to leave. But it was all in her bank account. Except for a little bit of holiday money he needed every so often, Dad never touched that money. At any given time, she was probably worth more financially than he was, as his Jamaican dollars were devaluing rapidly, but his US dollars (all in her name) were retaining their value. She was loving it. In fact, she used to gloat that she drove around in a super-duper, brand-new Honda, while her husband drove around a ten-year-old clunker back in Jamaica. This was only because he just did not care about what kind of car he drove, but to her it was very symbolic. She was financially secure and never had to beg him for money again.

It is quite ironic that the instability in Jamaica that we all initially resented ended up giving Mom a life of total stability that, needless to say, she thoroughly embraced. Maybe we should have thanked Michael Manley after all.

Mom lived out the last twenty-three years of her life in Houston. There she found herself on a more tranquil path, for sure, but what was important was that her challenging experiences in Jamaica had forced her to grow into a strong, independent woman. Did she miss her unpredictable life on that hot tropical island? Did she miss the hurricanes, the earthquakes, the insects, the fires, and the unbearable heat? Did she miss sitting on her veranda looking down onto the lights of Kingston, wondering where her philandering husband was? I do not believe so.

Although her life in Houston was not a fraction as spicy as her life in Jamaica, she had no regrets about her move. In fact, during the twenty-three years she lived in Houston, she returned to Ireland many times on visits, but she never once returned to Jamaica, the place she had called home for thirty years. Nor did she ever express a desire to. I guess she was quite happy to give up her hot peppery jerk chicken, especially when she realized that southern fried chicken was just as good, and better still, there was no heartburn that went along with it. Her heart had been burned too many times in Jamaica, and the painful memories far outweighed the good ones. It had been an interesting ride, but she was glad it was over.

There was only one thing that ever bothered her about living in Houston. Whenever we were out and she ordered whisky, straight up with a dash of water, she often got bourbon. *Oooh, not so tasty.* Once she remembered to specify, "Irish whiskey, that is," life was great.

Like Tony and I, Mom loved the United States. I truly do believe it is, and always will be, the greatest country in the world. As soon as we were able to, we took the test to become US citizens. We had embraced our new country, and it had embraced us. We had found a new sense of belonging that had been so brutally taken away from us in Jamaica. Unlike Mom though, I still visit Jamaica. After all, the crystal-blue waters and white sandy beaches are tantalizing. On a recent visit there, as I was driving across the country on a brand-new road from Kingston to Montego Bay, I was blown away by the beauty of the lush misty Blue Mountains and its many meandering rivers. I had forgotten how magnificent the vistas were. If only Houston had mountains. Oh well, you can't have everything I guess.

Today, I only travel to Jamaica as a tourist, knowing I can leave whenever I want and that I will always have the safety net of my US citizenship protecting me.

Dad, on the other hand, never became a citizen of the United States, because he never really emigrated from Jamaica. He remained there until the day he had a stroke at sixty-nine years of age. This happened while he was walking to his car after work. He just collapsed on the parking lot. The stroke completely paralyzed his left side. It was a terrible shock to him. He had been an athlete and a ladies' man, full of energy, and never sick a day in his life. He had certainly never been admitted to a hospital. And there he was, barely able to walk or eat. He did get some physical therapy that got him back to the stage of shuffling around a bit and eating without too much mess, but it was devastating to his psyche.

Naturally the young "lassie" he was living with at the time soon left him, and he found himself alone and totally unable to take care of himself. It was a huge blow to his ego and self-esteem.

Although Mom and I were both thinking, "Well, you sort of deserve this, Tom," we knew we could not leave my father in this state. I got on a plane and brought him to Houston. I think Mom went into a quiet state of panic at the thought of his living in Houston, but much to her relief, I insisted he live with me. I knew that was the last thing she wanted was to have to take care of Dad after a stroke. She could never have coped with him in a healthy state much less half paralyzed.

Dad lived with me and my long-suffering husband for twelve years until he died in 2005. He was never a burden and never complained. In fact, even though I could tell most of the time he was depressed, he was always in surprisingly good humor. But I knew this was not the way he wanted to spend the last years of his life. It was heartbreaking for me to watch. He did not make much effort to rehabilitate his body though I tried to get him to exercise. It was as if he just gave up. He spent his days watching TV, and most of his outings consisted of cheering on his grandchildren from the sidelines as they participated in whatever sport they were into at the time. In later years, he did this from a wheelchair.

I knew, deep down, in a dysfunctional way Mom sort of felt vindicated. She remained quite active and healthy all during the years my father was incapacitated. She may have had a little bit of sympathy for him (she did have a soft heart), but she loved the fact that now she had more energy than him. She loved having her independence and her freedom to drive anywhere she wanted, while he was totally dependent on either her or me to take him places. What a reversal of roles! What goes around comes around, as they say.

Mom remained healthy and active until the day she just dropped dead from a heart attack at the age of seventy-three. She was still living in Houston, and we still saw each other at least three times a week. She was a confidant, a friend, and always good company, and I miss her terribly.

I was devastated when she died—it was so sudden and unexpected. As I was arranging the funeral, Dad told me he wanted to see her before they closed the casket. I took him down to the funeral home, and he got out of his wheelchair and knelt down beside her coffin. I had pinned her favorite broach on her dress. It was a sparking miniature flag of the stars and stripes. I knew she would have liked that, as she really did love America. To my shock, as Dad leaned over her coffin, he started to weep uncontrollably. I had never ever seen my father cry before. This was totally unexpected and, of course, started a flood of tears streaming down my face too.

Then he said something that blew me away. For the first time I realized how truly remorseful he was about the wayward life he had led and the hell he had put my mother through while he was living it.

He knelt there, weeping and just staring at her lifeless body for a long time.

"She is still beautiful," he finally sobbed. There was a long pause and then he said, "She is going straight to heaven, and I am going straight to hell."

I don't know what got into me, but I just said, "Yes, Dad, that's probably true."

Sunset in Jamaica—The end of a journey
Photo©Cookie Kinkead

Printed in Great Britain
by Amazon

51796087R00108